christian
aid
We believe in life before death

Cleveland Circles
John E Eckersley
by John E Eckersley
£10.00

'Cleveland Circles' is the sixth walking guide produced by the York Christian Aid group and printed by York printers, The Max Design & Print co. If you have enjoyed this book, why not collect others in the set? All are available from John Eckersley, Heslington Vicarage, York YO10 5EE.

In each case, the price includes the cost of post and packaging. Cheques made payable to 'Christian Aid' please.

by Leslie Stanbridge
£5.50 (includes p&p)

enjoyed by both walkers and cyclists. From the Vale of York, the route crosses the North York Moors and then follows the Esk Valley down to Whitby.

The centre section of the book contains a route description for completing the Whitby Way by Cycle.

The **'Tidewater Way'** is a long-distance footpath across northern England, tidal water to tidal water, from Lancaster on the River Lune to Ulleskelf on the River Wharfe.

Thirty-two pages of full-colour, detailed, easy-to-use maps and clear illustrations guide walkers for 90 miles through Lancashire and the Yorkshire Dales.

£5.50 (includes p&p)

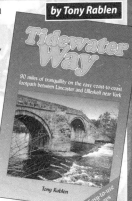
by Tony Rablen
Tidewater Way
90 miles of tranquility on the easy coast-to-coast footpath between Lancaster and Ulleskelf near York
Tony Rablen
Easy-to-use maps

'ECHOES' stands for English Counties Highest Original or Engineered Summits.

In this book, each of 40 ECHOES is included in a long walk of about ten miles and for the majority of these itineraries there is a shorter option of approximately five miles. Every May Bank Holiday the author co-ordinates Christian Aid walks to each of these 40 county summits.

ECHOES
or Eckoes?
by John E Eckersley
£9.00 (includes p&p)

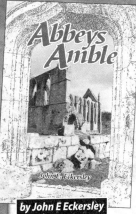
Abbeys Amble
John E. Eckersley
by John E Eckersley

'Abbeys Amble' is a 103-miles linear walk starting and finishing at Ripon Cathedral. It links up three famous Yorkshire Abbeys (Fountains, Bolton Priory and Jervaulx) as well as visiting three Yorkshire castle (Ripley, Bolton and Middleham). *Abbeys Amble* may be completed as a series of 24 day circular walks.

£9 (includes p&p)

Exploring Lake Pickering
John E. Eckersley
by John E Eckersley

John Eckersley's **'Lake Pickering Circuit'** is a 155-mile trail following the higher land around the edge of the former Lake Pickering.

The trail is made up of 36 separate walks which pass along the Howardian and Tabular Hills, the North Sea coastal cliffs and the Yorkshire Wolds.

£10.00 (includes p&p)

Cleveland Circles

by
John E. Eckersley

with
Mark Comer
Nancy Eckersley
Paul Ferguson
Peter Main
Daniel Savage

Aerial photographs by
Margaret & David Casson

© and Published by
John E. Eckersley 2006

ISBN 0 9535862 3 5

Printed by
The Max Design & Print Co., York, England

FOREWORD

AT THE BEGINNING of my ministry as Archbishop, I am looking forward to getting to know the countryside in the Diocese of York. My friends tell me that walking the Cleveland Way is one of the best ways of enjoying it, and how each of the seasons brings its own character and colours.

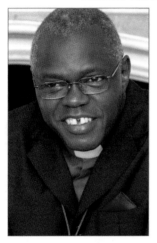

Many thousands follow the well-marked Cleveland Way itself: over the hilltops northwards from Helmsley, down to the sea at Saltburn, and then along the coast via Whitby and Scarborough to Filey.

But what about the places off the track? There are so many further interesting locations to see, and discoveries to make, when we dare to explore. So I am enormously grateful to John Eckersley for writing this book - not so much a guide to the Cleveland Way as a companion to fascinating detours, thirty *Cleveland Circles*. It is a book to inspire walkers in two senses - first so that we can enjoy the scenery, again and again experiencing new breathtaking vistas when we reach a turning or hillcrest; secondly because it opens our eyes to the story, and in particular the Christian story, of the people who have lived in this part of North-East England.

Sometimes John shows us ruins and ancient sites - in almost every walk he takes us to places where worship is still held regularly and faithfully. Still, let us not think even of the old sites as just historical curiosities but rather as a reminder that many men and women, most of whose names are unrecorded by human history, kept the Gospel alive in the communities, moorlands and farms of hillside and coast. Let your mind's eye take away the marks of the centuries on the landscape and imagine how you are seeing the same scenery as Hilda, Caedmon, Postgate and Wesley.

I do hope that you will enjoy using this book, and that you will have great pleasure as you discover more of the wonderful scenery, as well as the story of faith and hope, with the help of *Cleveland Circles*.

+Sentamu Ebor

Letter from Harrogate

I had a dream last night; a terrible dream; a haunting dream. I was visited by a ghostly apparition, an austere figure looking a bit like Methuselah was chasing me down the hillside in his size 10 hiking boots, clutching his books of wisdom and trying to hide his thinning top under a woolly bob-hat.

He caught me up and suddenly, I realised – it was John Eckersley in disguise! He'd come back to haunt me. Three long years after I'd written the Introduction to his last book for Christian Aid, he was pleading with me once more. Words, though, were never spoken. He just looked penetratingly through me ... but the vibes were clear. 'Tim, I'm desperate; I need your help again.' And then he vanished.

In a panic I woke. What should I do? After all, John's an old friend. I thought. Ah well, I suppose three years is a long time in book-writing ... I'll give it a go. Trouble was, what could I say that wasn't scurrilous, libellous or downright untrue?

Then an idea came. Simple. The truth. I'll just tell the embarrassing truth.

Those of you who've seen John's 'ECHOES (or Eckoes)' book will remember that all the best ideas for that publication came from his good wife Nancy. It's been exactly like that with 'Cleveland Circles'. Ever since John retired from teaching at St Aidan's, Nancy's had to find him things to do in order to keep him out of her way. 'Cleveland Circles' seemed a good idea. Their conversation went something like this:

'Darling, how about writing another walking book for Christian Aid? You know what wonderful work Christian Aid does.' 'Well, I've written several already; maybe I need a change and should be doing something else.'

'Just think; if you wrote a book, you'd have a perfect excuse for getting out in the fresh open air and all that walking you'd need to do would help keep you fit and stop you becoming a couch potato stuck in front of the telly all day.' 'Mmm ... maybe, but writing a book isn't as easy as it looks you know. There's an awful lot of hard work involved.'

'But you don't have to do all the work yourself. Remember, what you need to do is to delegate all the difficult bits to other people – just as you've done with the other books. So Mark can do the really hard graft converting your scribbled sketch plans into beautiful maps; Dan will do his superb line drawings; Margaret and David can go up in the plane to take the aerial shots and I'll draw the cartoons and take the photos for you. All you have to do is to put your name on the front cover – it couldn't be easier!' 'I must admit, when you put it like that the idea does sound tempting.'

'And to make it a real O.A.P. Special you could have a word with Tim and ask him to write a nice introduction for you – there you see, it's easy!' 'What a brilliant idea! Why didn't I think of that? When do I start?'

John's spectre still walks the corridors of St Aidan's. Those of us old enough to remember him recall the days of his madcap antics running all over the countryside supporting his charity runs for Christian Aid. But this time he's forgotten to ask me to sell the books, join the inaugural run, get sponsorship and cajole St Aidan's to become involved. Never mind, we'll still be there. Nancy's right; this is a real O.A.P. Special! Hope you enjoy it as much as we're going to!

Tim Pocock

Tim Pocock
*(An old friend of John's, but not as old as he is
Chairman St Aidan's C. of E. High School Charities Committee)*

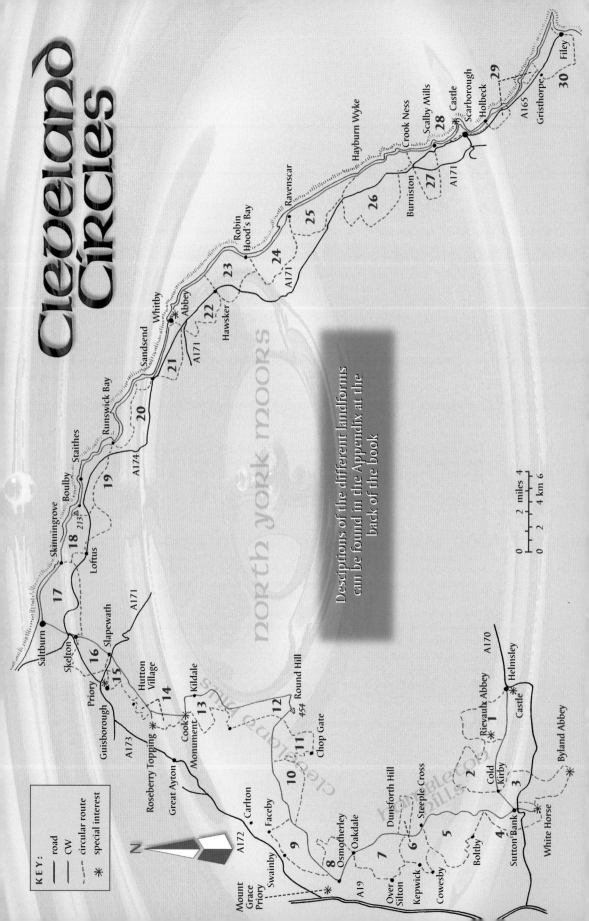

Cleveland Circles

KEY:
— road
CW
- - - circular route
* special interest

N

Descriptions of the different landforms can be found in the Appendix at the back of the book

0   2 miles 4
0   2   4 km 6

north york moors

Cleveland Hills

Hambleton Hills

Mount Grace Priory
A172
Swainby
Carlton
Faceby
Osmotherley
Oakdale
A19
Over Silton
Kepwick
Cowesby
Boltby
White Horse
Byland Abbey
Sutton Bank
Cold Kirby
Steeple Cross
Dunsforth Hill
Chop Gate
Round Hill
454
Castle
Helmsley
A170
Rievaulx Abbey
Great Ayton
Monument
Cook
Roseberry Topping
Kildale
Hutton Village
Guisborough
Priory
A173
Skelton
Saltburn
Slapewath
A171
Skinningrove
Boulby
Staithes
213?
Loftus
A174
Runswick Bay
Sandsend
Whitby
Abbey
A171
Hawsker
Robin Hood's Bay
A171
Ravenscar
Hayburn Wyke
Crook Ness
Burniston
Scalby Mills
Castle
Scarborough
Holbeck
A171
A165
Gristhorpe
Filey

1
2
3
4
5
6
7
8
9
10
11
12
13
14
15
16
17
18
19
20
21
22
23
24
25
26
27
28
29
30

CLEVELAND WAY & CLEVELAND CIRCLES
WALK DISTANCES

WALK LOCATIONS		CW DISTANCE (miles approx)	CW (TOTAL) (miles approx)	CIRCLE WALK (miles approx)	CIRCLES (TOTALS) (miles approx)
1	HELMSLEY – ASHBERRY FARM	3.2	3.2	11.2	11.2
2	ASHBERRY FAIRM – COLD KIRBY	2.6	5.8	11.9	23.1
3	COLD KIRBY – SUTTON BANK	2.4	8.2	12.9	36.0
4	SUTTON BANK – near BOLTBY	3.2	11.4	9.0	45.0
5	near BOLTBY – STEEPLE CROSS	3.7	15.1	10.1	55.1
6	STEEPLE CROSS – DUNSFORTH'S HILL	1.3	16.4	12.1	67.2
7	DUNSFORTH'S HILL – OAK DALE	3.7	20.1	10.4	77.6
8	OAK DALE – SOUTH WOOD	2.6	22.7	9.2	86.8
9	SOUTH WOOD – LIVE MOOR	3.8	26.5	10.2	97.0
10	LIVE MOOR – COLD MOOR	4.2	30.7	10.0	107.0
11	COLD MOOR – URRA MOOR	3.1	33.8	10.2	117.2
12	URRA MOOR – BATTERSBY MOOR	5.5	39.3	10.5	127.7
13	BATTERSBY MOOR – COOK'S MONUMENT	5.0	44.3	11.5	139.2
14	COOK'S MONUMENT – HIGHCLIFF NAB	4.6	48.9	10.4	149.6
15	HIGHCLIFF NAB – SLAPEWATH	3.5	52.4	10.3	159.9
16	SLAPEWATH – SKELTON	2.6	55.0	12.5	172.4
17	SKELTON – SKINNINGROVE	6.0	61.0	10.8	183.2
18	SKINNINGROVE – BOULBY	2.6	63.6	10.7	193.9
19	BOULBY – RUNSWICK BANK TOP	5.4	69.0	11.4	205.3
20	RUNSWICK BANK TOP – TELLGREEN HILL	4.0	73.0	8.8	214.1
21	TELLGREEN HILL – WHITBY	4.7	77.7	11.6	225.7
22	WHITBY – near HAWSKER	3.6	81.3	10.9	236.6
23	near HAWSKER – ROBIN HOOD'S BAY	3.7	85.0	9.2	245.9
24	ROBIN HOOD'S BAY – RAVENSCAR	3.1	88.1	10.8	256.6
25	RAVENSCAR – HAYBURN WYKE	4.3	92.4	11.0	267.6
26	HAYBURN WYKE – CROOK NESS	3.1	95.5	12.0	279.6
27	CROOK NESS – SCALBY MILLS	2.3	97.8	9.4	289.0
28	SCALBY MILLS – HOLBECK	3.9	101.7	8.5	297.5
29	HOLBECK – GRISTHORPE CLIFF	4.2	105.9	11.2	308.7
30	GRISTHORPE CLIFF – FILEY	2.7	108.6	10.0	318.7

The CW distances given above do not include the return walks along the two CW spurs of the White Horse and Roseberry Topping. These returns would add approximately an extra 1.8 miles to the total distance.

The slope profiles for each walk show the variations of height which can be expected along the route.

The Christian Heritage

The area covered in this book is rich in the Christian legacy left by people and their buildings. As we explore we may wish to ponder on our role in this evolving story. Figures in [brackets] refer to the numbered walks.

Before the Norman Conquest

The area's best-known saint is Hilda (died 680) who established a monastery with simple buildings at WHITBY [22] where, as Bede writes, the herdsman Caedmon received the gift of composing Anglo-Saxon religious poetry of unrivalled quality.

The Anglo-Saxon period saw the English Church suffer at the hands of the Vikings but there was also some peaceful merging of cultures. Sculptures and fragments at KIRBY KNOWLE [5], KILDALE [13], UPLEATHAM [16], LYTHE [21] and WHITBY come from a context influenced by Christianity. As for buildings, we can guess that many have disappeared without trace but we know that there were pre-Conquest churches at OLD BYLAND (wooden) [2], HACKNESS [close to 27] and possibly OSMOTHERLEY [8] and FILEY [30].

The Age of the Monasteries

The growth and ascendancy of the monasteries did most to shape the Christian history of North Yorkshire in the Middle Ages. Only a dozen years after the Norman Conquest, a monastery of Benedictines was re-founded at WHITBY. There was a Benedictine nunnery at ARDEN [6] and another of unknown order at FOULKEHOLM (now Nun House) south of Osmotherley [close to 7].

The Cistercians established RIEVAULX [1] in 1132 and nearby BYLAND [3]. BAYSDALE [close to 12] was a Cistercian community of nuns, built characteristically in a remote place. The Cistercians' influence was not restricted to their monastic buildings because they established granges or farms which were significant enterprises in land management and improvement; the place name 'grange' often persists to this day. Sites of granges include GRIFF [1], OLD BYLAND and MURTON to its north-west [2], Busby, Dromonby and the 'disappeared' settlement of Little Broughton on the flat land overlooked by the Cleveland Hills. They also operated a large fishing complex close to Byland.

Another distinctive presence was that of the Carthusians at Mount Grace and the Lady Chapel which they built a little way north of OSMOTHERLEY [8] remains a centre of prayer and pilgrimage and reminds us movingly of our monastic inheritance.

SCARBOROUGH [28] became a major centre of religious life and typified the pattern of religious activity in towns in England from the 13th century onwards. As well as the medieval parish church, there were communities of Franciscans, Carmelites and Dominicans living there. The friars' ministry was characterised by preaching, as they lived in holy poverty and were supported by gifts. The friars were also active in the countryside and there was a Carmelite friary at KILDALE [13].

Effects of the Reformation

The great Age of the Monasteries ended with their Dissolution by Henry VIII in the 1530s. All who were dependent on their economic activity felt the effects and the whole of Whitby town experienced a decline. Discontent, and loyalty to the old ways, were expressed in the Pilgrimage of Grace (1536) which was an ill-fated attempt to curb the programme of dissolution. Some of the participants marched westwards from the GUISBOROUGH area [15] to join others from Yorkshire and beyond. This was an indicator of the local religious climate, for throughout the time of the Reformation and for long after, many people in the area, both the gentry and the general population, were known to be Roman Catholics. In the 17th century sizeable numbers of Roman Catholics are recorded at such places as KIRBY KNOWLE [5], HAWNBY [close to 6], OSMOTHERLEY [8], LYTHE [21], WHITBY [21,22] and SCARBOROUGH [28]. Many priests who had attended seminaries abroad entered England via the discreet harbour of WHITBY. Of those who ministered in the area the best known is perhaps the martyred Nicholas Postgate (died 1678).

Puritanism did not have many adherents in this region, though in the late 17th century the Society of Friends gained strength. There was a Quaker cemetery serving the Whitby area from 1659 and a meeting house in ROBIN HOOD'S BAY [23] in 1690. Some Friends suffered for their principles. One Isaac Robinson refused to celebrate England's military victories with his neighbours and reportedly had his windows broken three times for his pains.

There are vivid records of John Wesley's visits to the area. He came to GUISBOROUGH nine times. At his visit on Midsummer Day in 1761 some of the people 'roared like the waves of the sea' to try to stop him being heard but he quietened the crowd enough to persuade many to attend another address at 5 a.m. the next day. A few years later, when he preached at Whitby, the church bells were rung to drown his voice – again unsuccessfully – and he was to make further visits, the last in 1788. The evangelistic work of John Wesley and his preachers was so effective that, added together, Methodists from the various strands of the movement soon made up the biggest number of worshipping Christians in the area.

The 18th and 19th Centuries

The buildings standing today give clues to changing patterns and priorities of church life and the architectural fashions that reflected them. But it is worth noting those churches where rebuilding seems to have enhanced their individual character, among them INGLEBY GREENHOW [12]. Another, the medieval SKELTON old church [16], was given a new nave in 1785. This building was mothballed a century later after a new church was built in the town centre in 1884.

By the mid-19th century about a quarter of the total population attended worship regularly. In this period the various denominations active in the area built a large number of chapels and churches. The Church of England constituted new parishes where population growth demanded it. There were some imaginative initiatives at that time, including the foundation of the Seamen's Mission near the fish quay in WHITBY, staffed by a Missioner and offering a chapel and reading room.

The 20th Century and our own time

The latter part of the 20th century witnessed increasing co-operation between different churches. If it is true that the building of trust is more important than trust in buildings, then we should not be ashamed when some buildings close but congregations unite in shared premises.

The churches of the Cleveland Circles area, like others elsewhere, still share a determination to serve the communities where they are set. St Peter's STAITHES [19] is an example of a building that has recently been adapted to make it more attractive and flexible, both for worship and for community use. As we walk around the countryside of the Cleveland Way, we are visiting places where the Christian message is alive and active. Many people are working hard to proclaim that Gospel afresh in this present age and to ensure that it is handed on to future generations.

Crosses and Stones of the North York Moors

The enigmatic Crosses on and around the edge of the North York Moors have long held a fascination for walkers. Some are true crosses with vertical shaft and horizontal crosspiece but others have only the shaft or the base stone remaining. Lewis Graham suggests the following five-fold classification and examples of these different Crosses can be found on Cleveland Circles walks.

Preaching Crosses are thought to have originated from the time when Celtic monks spread the Christian message through North Yorkshire and set up wooden or perhaps stone crosses from which to speak.

Memorial Crosses are believed to have been erected in memory of particular priests or monks who had been especially admired by their congregations.

Boundary Crosses or Stones indicate a division of property between adjacent landowners and may be found on prominent landmarks, such as a prehistoric tumulus, or at an important bend in the boundary line. Landowners indicated their territories by carving their initials into the stone.

Waymarker Crosses were invaluable in the days before O.S. maps and G.P.S. aids could help navigation across desolate moorlands and a sizeable number of moorland stones are the remnants of medieval waymarks. Confirmation that you were journeying in roughly the right direction must have been just as comforting to travellers in those days as it can be today. Those who voluntarily built the earlier waymarker crosses may have had genuine philanthropic motives but then in 1711 the Justices of Northallerton ordered that guide posts had to be erected at all the crossroads in the county.

Market Crosses marked the focus of both the economic and the social life of village communities. It has been said that the intention of the market crosses was to 'pay homage to Christ crucified and to remind men that there should be a sense of morality in their dealings in the market'. However, when the Puritans came to power in the 17th century they sometimes removed the crosses from the tops of the shafts and replaced them with balls such as we see today at Guisborough. Public announcements could be made from the village cross and it could also be used as a base for outdoor preaching. This was especially the case where the cross was mounted on a substantial plinth.

In 1971 Malcolm Boyes pioneered a 53 miles circuit linking 13 of the moorland crosses. However, none of these 13 crosses is visited on the 30 Cleveland Circles walks in this book. Instead, some of the lesser known crosses can be sought out, though in some cases their remains are not easy to find. Wherever possible, each walk has its own cross but on those walks where there is no cross I have substituted some other kind of special stone that has particular significance for that walk. Photos of these special Treasure Hunt clues appear in the centre pages of the book and readers are encouraged to see how many of these they can find – a key for their identification is given along with the other Treasure Hunt locations at the end of the book.

WALK 1 HELMSLEY – ASHBERRY FARM

Map: Explorer OL 26
S.E.P.T.: Helmsley car park (611838)
Buses: 128,195,196,197, M4, M7, M8, M13, M15
Cleveland Way distance: **3.2 miles**
Circular walk distance: **11.2 miles**
Shorter walk alternative: **5.5 miles**
Special interest:
   Rievaulx Abbey, St Mary's Church, Helmsley Castle and Church, Griff
Cross: Helmsley Market Cross (612838)

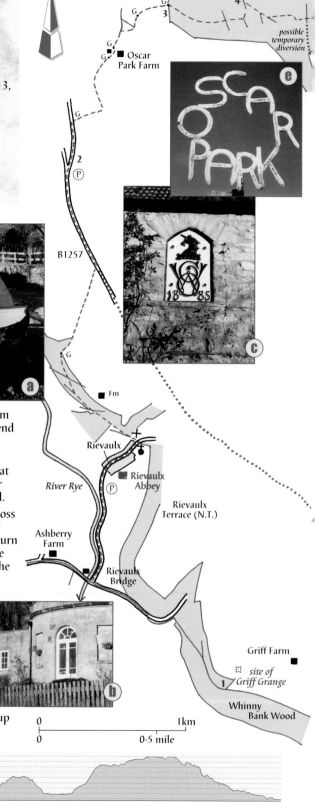

The first of the Cleveland Circles Walks offers the opportunity to visit Rievaulx Abbey as well as Helmsley's Castle and Church. Other less well-known attractions include the site of Griff medieval grange, St Mary's Church and Rievaulx Bridge Cottage.

The longer walk starts and finishes at Helmsley car park. Use of compass (and a little boldness) may be helpful for about 600m when crossing into Beck Dale at the northern end of the walk.

If two cars are available, a shorter walk can be arranged by parking a second car in the lay-by at the road junction (2) and using this to transfer walkers back to Helmsley along the B1257 road.

The Cleveland Way officially starts at the old cross in the town's market square, so in order to say that we have walked all of the CW we have to turn right out of the car park, then right again at the Stokesley road before bending left in front of the parish church to reach the market cross. Our mileage measurement starts from here.

Returning to the car park, we follow the Cleveland Way westwards out of the town. The route is clearly identified by the National Trail acorn symbols. It is worth pausing to look back at Helmsley Castle as we rise gradually towards Blackdale Howl Wood.

Soon we pass Griff Lodge and then come to the permissive access path on our right (1) up to the site of the deserted medieval grange of Griff.

Descending steeply through Quarry Bank Wood, we turn left when we reach the road and shortly come to

Rievaulx Bridge. At this point, if we wish to claim that we have walked all the Cleveland Way, we need to do a short out-and-back diversion to Ashberry Farm (since this stretch of road will not be included on the next walk) before we turn northwards on the road to Rievaulx Abbey.

The Abbey deserves full attention – some may wish to come on a separate visit rather than make a rushed call to this exceptionally beautiful piece of our national heritage. However, whether we enter the Abbey now or at a later time, we should make certain to look in at St Mary's Church a little further along the road.

Turning right as we leave the church, we quickly come to the Methodist

we use the wide grass verge to bring us to the lay-by (2) where the shorter walk party may have left some of their cars to transport them back to Helmsley. The longer walk continues on the roadside to the path turn-off to Oscar Park Farm.

The farm track leads us through Oscar Park farmyard and then, by a solitary sycamore tree about 100m further on, the p.r.o.w. swings right up to a fence. Here we turn left and soon go through the waymarked gate before bending right along the field edge.

When we enter the trees (3) we see two tracks; we use the waymarked one going straight ahead and follow a wide, sometimes muddy, route through the wood. In autumn, there is a fine variety of colourful fungi – as bright as any you could find in a child's book of fairy tales. We swing round left to the track junction at (4), turn sharp right, and then at the fingerpost about 120m further on, branch off left from the main track on to a narrow path up into the trees.

The path twists right, right again and then left before we hit a major forest drive running at right angles to our route. The p.r.o.w. goes straight over into the trees and on to a second wide forest track. Again crossing straight over, the narrow path descends steeply on a springy bed of conifer needles to the bottom of Beck Dale (5). Expect a surprise; this valley and its clear stream are a real delight.

The steps on the other side of the water lead us up to the top of the valley side. Turning right for 100m or so, we then stay up on the earth track just inside the trees, rather than using the broader track going down the slope (6). However, after another few hundred metres, a fingerpost (7) directs us sharp right and we take this route down to the valley floor. From then the track is obvious, criss-crossing from side to side of the beck. This is such a lovely valley I am amazed it's not more popular.

At the confluence of valleys where Etton Gill joins in (8), we follow the fingerpost and bear left to walk parallel to the stream now known as Borough Beck. A little way past the sawmill, we take the right fork in the track (9), cross a stone footbridge and follow the paved path back to Helmsley.

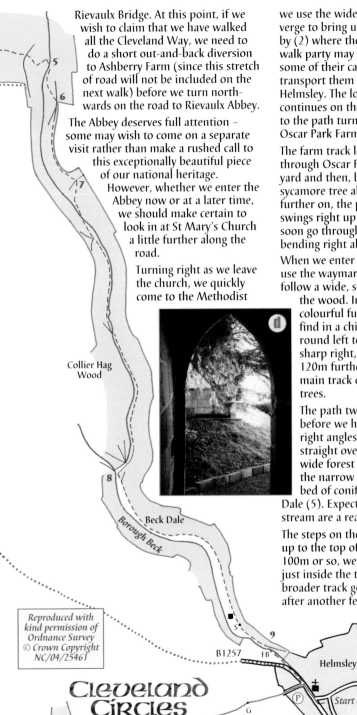

Collier Hag Wood

Beck Dale

Borough Beck

Cleveland Circles

steps

Blackdale Howl Wood

B1257   FB

Helmsley

P   Start of CW

Castle

RYEBURN ICE CREAM PARLOUR and TEA ROOM

Chapel on our left and follow the tarmac way leading off left. Avoiding cross-paths, our route continues through the trees and then bends right to climb gently up to the B1257 road. Turning left,

Special Interest – WALK 1

Rievaulx Abbey, the first of four superb medieval Cistercian abbeys built in North Yorkshire, was founded in 1132 on land granted by the Norman lord Walter l'Espec. The Cistercians have been described as an international movement of monastic hardliners, every detail of their lives being carefully regulated in order to preserve their strict regime. They acted as a kind of reform movement, wanting to recapture something of the zeal of the early Benedictine monks who had originally turned their backs on an easy, comfortable life. So the Cistercians chose to settle in inhospitable areas away from towns, aiming to adopt lives of poverty and austerity. For the first time 'lay brothers' were included in the monastic community. These men followed a modified monastic regime and were also responsible for the labouring jobs in the abbey.

The Cistercians were expected to be self-supporting and as the monasteries increased in size more land was given to them by their benefactors. These gifts included lands in Bilsdale, the Vale of Mowbray, Ryedale and the Vale of Pickering so it was necessary for the lay brothers to build additional farms at these locations. Rievaulx, the most important Cistercian monastery in Britain, had some 20 of these farms, or granges, in Yorkshire. Sheep farming was especially important and at one time the Rievaulx monks owned 14,000 sheep. They also operated their own fishery at Teesmouth, developed iron mining in Bilsdale and Wakefield and built what are perhaps the oldest industrial canals in England.

Increasing prosperity enabled the monks to make lavish extensions to their buildings and the plain character of the early church changed to the more elaborate and imaginative style of the early English Gothic period. Details of the monastery's development can be obtained from the excellent audio guide available at the information desk.

Rievaulx's most famous monk was **St Aelred**. He came from the court of King David of Scotland and had risen to the rank of king's steward, before suddenly deciding that he should abandon his secular prospects and join the abbey community at Rievaulx. Aelred is remembered for his idea of 'Spiritual Friendship'. He made what was at the time the daring suggestion that, just as the Bible states, 'God is Love' so one might also say, 'God is Friendship'. The monastic tradition had previously been mistrustful of friendship, wary that friendships could create factions and so destroy the authority of the abbot and the unity of the abbey fellowship. Although an abbot himself, Aelred seems to have been unperturbed about possible challenges to his leadership through 'spiritual friendships'.

Griff For many years it was assumed that the 'humps and bumps' on the landscape west of Griff Farm were the remains of a medieval village, as labelled on the O.S. map. However, a detailed investigation of the site was carried out by English Heritage in December 2002 and the findings of this survey have shown that most of the remains form part of one of the granges which belonged to Rievaulx Abbey. Little evidence of a village was discovered.

St Mary's Church The nave of St Mary's Church was originally the Gate Chapel of Rievaulx Abbey but in 1538 during Henry VIII's Dissolution of the Monasteries both Abbey and Gate Chapel were 'slighted' and had to be surrendered to the king. The chapel, located between what were the outer and inner gates of the Abbey, stood derelict until the Earl of Feversham funded its reconstruction and extension in 1906-1907. The outer gate lay across the road where cottages now stand and would have had a wide archway with folding doors and a small lodge for the porter.

Things to look for outside the church building include the 'Rievallens' inscription on the north-west corner buttress and, at the roadside, the stone base of the main gate archway. One of the treasures inside the church is the tapestry showing Christ's journey to his crucifixion.

Helmsley Castle was probably built originally in the early 12th century by Walter l'Espec, the founder of Rievaulx Abbey and Kirkham Priory. However, the oldest parts of the castle we see today date from the time of Robert de Roos (known as 'Fursan') who was Lord of Helmsley from about 1186 to 1227.

One of the special features of Helmsley Castle is the double-ditch defence created to help protect

Helmsley Castle

Dan Savage

the fortification. Double ditches like these are unique in Yorkshire and rare in England. One authority goes as far as describing the embankment between the ditches as 'the noblest thing of its kind in England' and another writer points out that to cut two ditches was 'a closely guarded royal right'. It is a puzzle as to who cut these ditches; they may have been constructed by Robert de Mortain before l'Espec, or by l'Espec himself, or by Fursan. They may even possibly have been dug at different times.

Robert Fursan is thought to have erected the curtain wall with its rounded towers and the eastern keep. (He built in white limestone, while later extensions used brown sandstone.) Round towers gave a wider field of fire for defensive crossbows and their shape also helped to deflect projectiles aimed at the defenders. Later alterations to the castle included the addition of barbicans to protect the north and south gates because it was from these directions that the fortress was entered in medieval times. Today we approach from the eastern side. Other modifications were the raising of the height of the eastern keep and the conversion of the western tower into residential quarters.

Helmsley Castle had a relatively uneventful history during the Middle Ages and there is no record of its having been captured or besieged until the time of the Civil War. Then in 1644 the Royalists under Sir Jordan Crosland were trapped in against a determined Parliamentary force until the castle was forced to capitulate and negotiate an honourable surrender. The Roundheads then slighted the castle and made it unusable.

All Saints Church, Helmsley retains its Norman south doorway and chancel arch although the building was almost entirely reconstructed (1866-1869) by the Victorians. Various aspects of church history are immediately visible in the stained glass and modern mural paintings, but the guidebook advises us to look carefully so that we 'do not miss the dragon, the mice and the slave's yoke'.

Helmsley Market Cross stands on a plinth of six steps, the slender shaft supporting a modern crosspiece. The cross originally stood in the churchyard. Today it is rather overshadowed by the ornately carved memorial to the Second Baron Feversham.

WALK 2
ASHBERRY FARM – COLD KIRBY

Map: Explorer OL 26
S.E.P.: Cold Kirby (533845)
Buses: M8 to Rievaulx
Cleveland Way distance: **2.6 miles**
Circular walk distance: **11.9 miles**
Shorter walk alternative: **7.0 miles**
Special interest:
  Cold Kirby and Old Byland Churches,
  Ashberry Wood Nature Reserve, Caydale SSSI
Cross or Stone: Sundial at All Saints Church, Old
  Byland (551859)

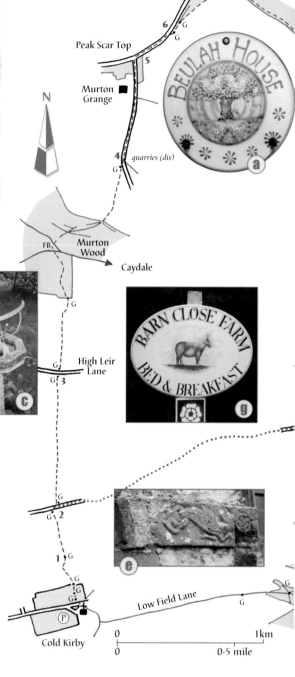

The full circuit for this walk includes a visit to Old Byland and, although this adds a couple of extra miles to the medium distance route, the diversion is highly recommended.

From the village green in Cold Kirby we go ENE and take the signposted p.r.o.w. leading through Ailred Barn. We pass through three gates and then down and up across a small depression to the gate at (1).

The bridleway follows the right side of the hedge to the road at (2) and here the shorter walk turns right and takes the road into Old Byland. The longer walk, offset to the right, continues north along the field-side to High Leir Lane at (3). With another right-left shuffle we carry on to the scrubby hawthorn wood ahead – this is part of the Caydale SSSI.

We descend on a steep narrow path to the valley floor where there's a marshy mix of springs and streamlets but the footbridge avoids the wettest parts and then we climb up the other side of the valley.

We follow the fingerposts for Murton, bearing right at the track crossing and then when we eventually reach the top of the valley side, turning left along the stone wall. Where the field-side track comes to the minor road (4), we continue north towards Murton Grange. Then a short way past the farm, we come to the road junction at (5).

Turning right we walk along the road to the bend where a bridleway bears off right through a gate (6). At another gate 150m further on the p.r.o.w. forks right again. We take this clear path for 1.5 miles walking just inside the edge of Cliff Wood and East Ley Wood.

At the track meeting point by a disused building (7) we continue ahead for 100m and then bend right, staying on the main track. After another 100m there is a sharp right turn at the track crossing

and then after 90m we steer left to a small gate and fingerpost at the wall corner. From here we follow the field edge and indicators that direct us down to Barnclose Farm.

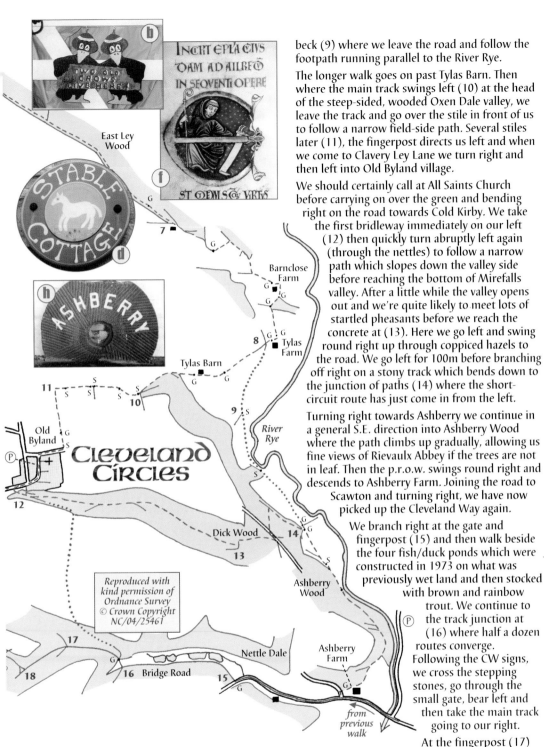

INCIT EPLA CIVS OAM AD AILBE IN SEQVENTI OPERE

ST OSWSTRIFS

Cleveland Circles

Reproduced with kind permission of Ordnance Survey © Crown Copyright NC/04/25461

beck (9) where we leave the road and follow the footpath running parallel to the River Rye.

The longer walk goes on past Tylas Barn. Then where the main track swings left (10) at the head of the steep-sided, wooded Oxen Dale valley, we leave the track and go over the stile in front of us to follow a narrow field-side path. Several stiles later (11), the fingerpost directs us left and when we come to Clavery Ley Lane we turn right and then left into Old Byland village.

We should certainly call at All Saints Church before carrying on over the green and bending right on the road towards Cold Kirby. We take the first bridleway immediately on our left (12) then quickly turn abruptly left again (through the nettles) to follow a narrow path which slopes down the valley side before reaching the bottom of Mirefalls valley. After a little while the valley opens out and we're quite likely to meet lots of startled pheasants before we reach the concrete at (13). Here we go left and swing round right up through coppiced hazels to the road. We go left for 100m before branching off right on a stony track which bends down to the junction of paths (14) where the short-circuit route has just come in from the left.

Turning right towards Ashberry we continue in a general S.E. direction into Ashberry Wood where the path climbs up gradually, allowing us fine views of Rievaulx Abbey if the trees are not in leaf. Then the p.r.o.w. swings round right and descends to Ashberry Farm. Joining the road to Scawton and turning right, we have now picked up the Cleveland Way again.

We branch right at the gate and fingerpost (15) and then walk beside the four fish/duck ponds which were constructed in 1973 on what was previously wet land and then stocked with brown and rainbow trout. We continue to the track junction at (16) where half a dozen routes converge. Following the CW signs, we cross the stepping stones, go through the small gate, bear left and then take the main track going to our right.

At the fingerpost (17) we bend left into Flassen Dale but soon need to turn right up the narrow valley (18). Soon the CW swings left and when we emerge from the trees at the top of the gulley, we have less than a mile of gentle climb on a wide track taking us towards Cold Kirby. Just before the village a narrow path on the right leads us back to our start.

The tarred track beyond Barnclose leads to Tylas Farm, about 0.3 mile further on. Rising up from Tylas, we come to a track crossing (8). Here the long itinerary goes straight over and through the gate on a stony track up towards Tylas Barn and then on to Old Byland. However, if we decide to miss out Old Byland, we turn left on the tarmac bridleway and go as far as the small Oxen Dale

Dan Savage

Rievaulx Abbey

CLEVELAND CIRCLES

Special Interest – WALK 2

St Michael's Church, Cold Kirby The present building was erected around 1841-1842 and replaced a much older structure dating back to the 12th century. The font is still the original one from the 12th century and one of the two bells dates from the 13th century. At first the parish was administered by the Knights Templars and later when they were suppressed, the Knights Hospitallers assumed control and they held the parish until the Reformation. Today Cold Kirby forms part of the Upper Ryedale parish along with four other churches.

Inside the church an information sheet describes the rather unedifying story of James Tankerlay, a medieval Byland monk who was priest for Cold Kirby. According to the story, his ghost caused consternation in the village and so his dead body and coffin were exhumed, carried to Gormire Lake and then thrown into the water.

All Saints Church, Old Byland has a Saxon sundial placed upside down on the east wall of the tower. The sundial is very rare as it has only ten divisions instead of the usual twelve and the inscription suggests possible Scandinavian connections. The church was rebuilt about 1145 by the Savignian monks from Furness Abbey when they were granted land at 'Bellalanda' (Byland) by Roger de Mowbray. Human heads with rams' horns decorate the Norman chancel arch and winged dragons guard the church porch.

Caydale SSSI was notified as a Site of Special Scientific Interest in July 2004. Caydale is a steep-sided valley and supports a range of different unimproved habitats in a relatively small area. Habitats range from mosaics of calcareous grassland and scrub to wetter habitats on the valley sides and floor. The wetter areas include fen-meadow as well as topogenous and soligenous mires. Topogenous mires develop where water collects in hollows in the landscape, as on the valley floor, and soligenous mires grow where water comes out of the valley side as a spring or flush.

Caydale possesses a nationally important population of Duke of Burgundy butterfly which is here at the most northerly extent of its natural range. The large area of mixed-age scrub and species-rich calcareous grassland forms essential habitat for this butterfly. Nationally the species is declining and so its protection here is regarded as a priority. Also significant is the population of brown argus butterflies. Several nationally rare beetles that depend on dead wood for their survival are likewise important.

In order to maintain its biological diversity, Caydale requires careful management. The grassland areas, for example, need sensitive grazing to prevent the land being taken over by rank grasses which would stop other species from growing. Some light trampling by animals can also be helpful in breaking down leaf litter and providing bare soil patches for seed germination.

Joseph Foord's 1763 Water Race channelled water 3.4 miles down Caydale valley to supply Old Byland. We cross the line of the old channel close to the 'Captain's Seat'.

Caydale Mill dates back to before 1598. It was dismantled in 1928 but the waterwheel was rebuilt to provide hydro-electric power.

Ashberry Nature Reserve is managed by Yorkshire Wildlife Trust and contains what the Trust describes as 'undoubtedly the finest ancient semi-natural woodland in central Yorkshire' as well as a range of mires, flushes and grasslands supporting a rich variety of flora and fauna. In this sense, the reserve has similarities with Caydale SSSI. The clay soils of the valley floor contrast with sandstones and limestones higher up the valley sides and this variation helps to account for the variety of habitats in the area. Bird's-eye primrose is a special attraction but as well as its colourful wild flowers the reserve has recorded more than 60 bird species. Red, fallow and roe deer are known to visit the woods.

(Note the reserve only contains a small part of Ashberry Wood itself, though it includes several other woods, and the 'main aim of management is to maintain and improve the diverse *grassland* flora and fauna'.)

Stone: Saxon sundial at All Saints Church, Old Byland

WALK 3
COLD KIRBY –
SUTTON BANK

Map: Explorer OL 26
S.E.P.T.: National Park Visitor Centre (516831)
Buses: 128, M2, M3
Cleveland Way distance: **2.4 miles**
Circular walk distance: **12.9 miles**
Shorter walk alternatives: **9.2 miles**
6.8 miles

Special interest:
  Byland Abbey, Scotch Corner, Mount
  Snever, Scawton Church, Hambleton Inn
Cross: Scawton Cross (549836)

There are shorter, medium and longer length walks for this section. All start from the Sutton Bank National Park Visitor Centre and all leave the CW part of the walk to the end. The main attraction of the longer walk is that it allows a visit to be made to Byland Abbey.

Leaving the Visitor Centre we walk east along the A170 to the minor road at (1). The short walk carries straight on before turning off along the minor road to Scawton but the medium and longer routes turn right and go as far as the bend at (2). Here we turn 90° left and follow the broad earth track which soon bends right before entering High Wood. We avoid the track going left at (3) and keep straight on down to Scotch Corner. A right-left zigzag is needed here but don't miss the tiny chapel on our right.

We carry on downwards along the earthen track and then at the tarmac footpath (4) those doing the medium distance walk turn back left on this

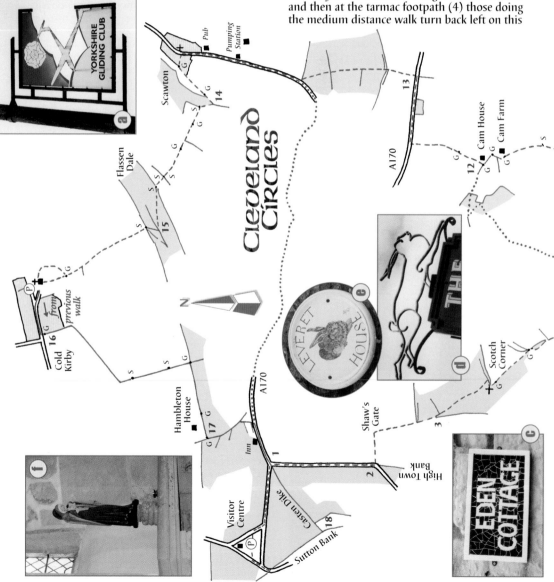

route leading to Cam Farm. Those opting for the longer circuit bear right and walk to the road ahead, where we turn left into Oldstead. We continue through the settlement to the Black Swan pub and here take the left road fork.

Soon we turn right (5) on another tarmac p.r.o.w. that takes us to Oldstead Grange. The route is waymarked through the farm and another sign directs us through a gate and we carry on down the farm track to cross a ditch. Immediately we are directed left (just inside the trees). When we come out of the trees, we stay by the field edge

Turning left, we take the track up into the woods. At the kissing gate (9) we take the centre path directing us to Cam Farm and the Observatory. The track climbs gradually, veering left and then right before reaching a clearing at the top of the slope (10). We turn right and walk to the wall at the edge of the wood (11). A concessionary path takes us left past Camp Holes, then left again after 200m, to the viewpoint at Mount Snever Observatory.

Returning to (11), we follow the wall-side path towards Cam Farm. As we approach the farm, we aim for the gate at the left end of the buildings and waymarks direct us round the farm over to Cam House (12). Here the medium distance walk joins in. At Cam House we must turn sharp right (at the time of writing there is no waymark on the first gate) and then, two fields later, we come to the main A170 road.

Turning right for about 400m on the grass verge, we come to the track crossing at (13). We turn left, cross the road and walk on into the wood. At the end of the trees, we go right on the road and come into Scawton.

Noting the remains of Scawton Cross outside the church perimeter wall, we should also look inside the church before we take the path by the telephone box just before the church. At the second gate we bend left along the grass farm track that leads to another gate before taking us down into a narrow gulley (14). We turn back right on ourselves and then soon swing left over a stile and follow waymarks along the field edges across towards Flassen Dale.

Entering the trees, the path bears left and then slopes down to the wide track in the bottom of the valley (15). We must now go left for about 25m. Here the p.r.o.w. goes up through the scrub and bramble to a stile at the top of the slope. From the top of the valley side it is about half a mile over farmland into Cold Kirby.

We now join the Cleveland Way at the village green. The Trail goes left through the settlement and then left again on a wide, signposted, track (16). This is known as Cote Moor Road and twists round to the edge of the Cote Moor forest. Here we turn sharp right along the edge of the wood and then pass between horse paddocks to the driveway just past Hambleton House (17).

A left turn takes us back to the A170 and then a right turn brings us to the road junction at (1) where we branched off earlier on the walk. This time we follow the CW direction through the trees and along the line of the ancient Casten Dike. When we reach the White Horse track (18) we turn right and walk back to our start.

and then turn sharp left (6) following the direction to Byland Abbey. Climbing a stile, we pass in front of Cams Head and continue towards the Abbey. Waymarks lead us over more stiles until we come to the minor road at (7). Turning left, the Abbey remains are immediately next to the roadside.

We follow the road round as far as the driveway to Abbey House, turn into the drive and then quickly go over the stile on our right. Following the footpath diagonally over two fields we come to a gate, by a seat, in the far corner at the top of the second field. Two more gates bring us to the edge of Wass village (8).

Reproduced with kind permission of Ordnance Survey © Crown Copyright NC/04/25461

Special Interest – WALK 3

The **Hambleton Inn** stands on the old Drovers Road from Scotland and has a proud record as a centre connected with horse-racing. The origins of racing at Hambleton are obscure but a diary entry of 1612 refers to an early contest and during the 17th and 18th centuries the Hambleton plateau racecourse was second in importance only to Newmarket. Although access to the course was not particularly easy, it had the advantage of a natural three-mile stretch of flat turf. The winning post, a stone obelisk with a sundial, was at the Dialstone Inn. Although racing moved to York and Richmond in 1776, the area still continues as a racehorse training ground today.

Hambleton Drove Road ('Hambleton Street') is an ancient highway, though some question whether it dates back as far as prehistoric times. It was much used in the 17th and 18th centuries for moving huge numbers of cattle and sheep from Scotland to England in order to supply fresh meat to the expanding English industrial towns. After crossing the Hambleton Hills the road split at the Hambleton Inn with one branch going east to Malton and the other going south to York. However, in the late 18th century, the lords of Oldstead established a turnpike and attempted to charge drovers a toll fee for passing through Oldstead Township. The drovers then changed their route and instead went down High Town Bank where no tolls were demanded. As we walk from Shaw's Gate to Oldstead we follow the route of the old Drove Road.

Scotch Corner was one of the Scottish drovers' stopping points where an inn and farmstead allowed rest and recuperation for both men and animals. The settlement fell into ruin but in the 1950s John Bunting, a teacher from Ampleforth College, created a small chapel to commemorate former students from the College who had been killed in World War II. Sadly, the chapel has suffered from periodic vandalism.

The **Battle of Byland** fought in 1322 has long been associated with Scotch Corner. Edward II, retreating with his English forces from Scotland, was heavily defeated by Robert Bruce and his pursuing Scottish army. Historians are uncertain of the exact site of the battle but it has been suggested that if the Scots marched from Northallerton, Sutton Bank itself would have been an obvious place for Edward to defend. When the first assault by the Scots up Sutton Bank was repulsed by the English rolling boulders down on them, the Scottish troops climbed the easier route from the south and attacked from the point still called Scotch Corner.

Mount Snever Observatory was built by John Wormald of Oldstead Hall in the first year of Queen Victoria's reign. Originally it had two floors and stairs leading to the rooftop. The verse which is carved above the outside door is a re-phrasing of part of Alexander Pope's 'Windsor Forest' poem.

Camp Holes is an intriguing set of trenches located to the east of the Observatory. Suggestions have been made that the trenches might be prehistoric defence works but they are unlike other ancient earthworks. Perhaps more plausible is the idea that they are the remains of medieval quarrying and are connected with the building of Byland Abbey. Although the stone is not especially good building material, it could have been used as rough stone for wall-filling or

Byland Abbey

for making lime. Hugh quantities of lime would have been required for the Abbey and there are remains of several limekilns in the area.

The Byland Trail In 1134 a group of Savignian (later to become Cistercian) monks left Furness Abbey to establish a new house at Calder. When after three years Scottish marauders had made life unbearable for them, they returned to their parent house at Furness. But the monks there would not take them in because the migrants refused to surrender their independence and so for a year they wandered homeless with all their worldly goods piled high on a single wagon pulled by eight oxen. Then they were granted land from the de Mowbray family on which they could establish themselves. At first they set up at Hood Grange below Sutton Bank and then, as their numbers grew, the de Mowbrays gave them more land at Old Byland ('Bellalanda'). Close by, at Tylas, they set up a tile making industry.

However, things at the Old Byland location were not going too well; the monks' bells clashed with those of nearby Rievaulx Abbey and the Furness monks were obliged to move once more. This time they settled at Stocking, now the village of Oldstead ('the old place' formerly used by the monks). Here they built a small church and living quarters. As we enter Oldstead on Walk 3, we see an avenue of trees leading to Oldstead Hall and on the left of the avenue lie the remains of the church and grange.

Gradually the community became more wealthy through other gifts of land and whilst at Stocking lay brothers were sent to drain the land at Byland and there they built the largest Cistercian church in Yorkshire.

Some of the special treasures of Byland include the large areas of fine floor tiles but the most dramatic remnant is the spectacular rose window in the west wall. The setting sun streaming through stained glass windows must have been an inspiring sight.

The monks of Byland and Newburgh had a complex system of waterworks which, as well as providing ponds for fishing, also made available waterpower for industry. To the left of the footpath which we follow from Oldstead Grange is the remains of a channel which carried water to Byland. Though most of the course is lost under cultivation, we see remains of the waterworks just before we reach the Abbey in the field marked 'Pond Bay' on the O.S. map.

St Mary's Church, Scawton The basic shape of the original building is unchanged. The font was brought from Old Byland Church in 1146 and has been used for baptisms since that time. Behind the 16th century communion table is the original stone altar with its small crosses on the corners. Stone altars were outlawed at the time of the Reformation, so this example is a rare treasure. Along the north wall is an unusual pillared sink that may have been brought from Byland or Rievaulx after the Dissolution of the Monasteries.

By the late 19th century the building needed considerable restoration and then again in 1999-2001 further work was undertaken as a result of a millennium appeal.

Scawton Cross: Outside St Mary's church wall is the stone base of the medieval wayside cross. Part of the missing shaft has apparently been used to make steps at a nearby farmhouse. It has been suggested that the cross might perhaps be the same age as the church (1146). The cross would have stood near Sperragate, the ancient road that ran from Helmsley to Thirsk.

WALK 4
SUTTON BANK –
near BOLTBY

Map: Explorer OL 26
S.E.P.T.: National Park Visitor Centre (516831)
Buses: 128, M2, M3
Cleveland Way distance: **3.2 miles**
Circular walk distance: **9.0 miles**
Shorter walk alternatives:
     North Loop **4.7 miles**
     South Loop **5.9 miles**
Special interest:
     Prehistoric remains, White Horse, Garbutt
     Wood, Gormire Lake, Hood Hill
Cross: Cooper's Cross (515829)

The route description starts from the Visitor Centre at Sutton Bank where we finished Walk 3 but it is also possible to use the Kilburn Woods free car park at the foot of the White Horse and so get the steep climb out of the way at the start of the walk.

We pick up the CW trail by the Talking Telescope (1) with its stunning views over the Vale of York and then we follow the wooded path along the top of Sutton Brow. A path down left (2) to Garbutt Wood Nature Reserve and Gormire Lake is the route for the shorter walk but the longer circuit continues along the scarp top round Whitestone Cliff and above South Woods.

About 150m after the bridleway leading off to Hambleton Road, we reach a clump of four hawthorn bushes on our left at (3) and here we

have a choice of route. If we wish to link up with the next circuit (Walk 5) we need to carry on a little way to the fingerpost at (4) directing us to Boltby. We go down as far as the gate, but instead of continuing down to Boltby, turn back left and follow the path just inside the wood and adjacent to the boundary wall to the gate at (5). This is a p.r.o.w. but has the big disadvantage of being poorly maintained.

The alternative is to take the better path down from (3) to the wood but this will mean that next time we will have to do an out-and-back link between (4) and (3) in order to say that we have completed all the Cleveland Way.

Whichever we choose, we follow the bridleway into the trees from the gate at (5). Almost immediately we swing left and continue down to meet a cross-track where we turn back right for 20m before cutting off left again down through the wood. Emerging at the gate on the edge of the wood, we stand with backs to the trees to spot the waymarked post diagonally ahead (between 10.00 and 11.00 o'clock direction) and then follow more waymarks across rough pasture (with lots of thistles) towards Southwoods Hall. The p.r.o.w. has been diverted around the hall and we are led over the driveway through another gate and on to the grassy path at (6).

We turn left, continue to the road crossing and then go straight ahead on the wide track into the trees. At Southwoods Lodge (7) we turn left and, avoiding two tracks off left to Thirlby Bank, bend right and continue towards Gormire. The pleasant, perhaps muddy, path takes us to a small triangle of paths at the far end of Gormire Lake (8) and here we go right towards Cleaves.

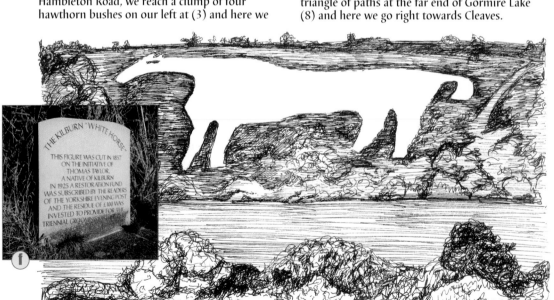

The Kilburn White Horse

Dan Savage

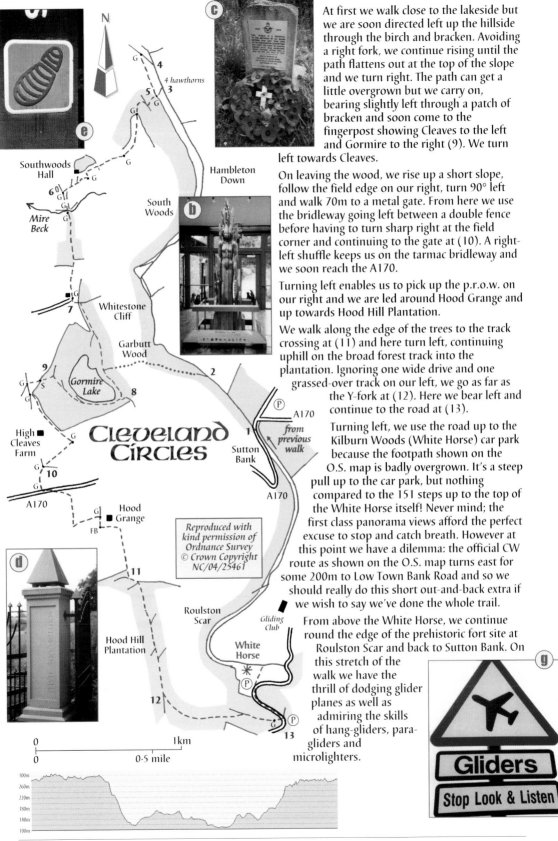

At first we walk close to the lakeside but we are soon directed left up the hillside through the birch and bracken. Avoiding a right fork, we continue rising until the path flattens out at the top of the slope and we turn right. The path can get a little overgrown but we carry on, bearing slightly left through a patch of bracken and soon come to the fingerpost showing Cleaves to the left and Gormire to the right (9). We turn left towards Cleaves.

On leaving the wood, we rise up a short slope, follow the field edge on our right, turn 90° left and walk 70m to a metal gate. From here we use the bridleway going left between a double fence before having to turn sharp right at the field corner and continuing to the gate at (10). A right-left shuffle keeps us on the tarmac bridleway and we soon reach the A170.

Turning left enables us to pick up the p.r.o.w. on our right and we are led around Hood Grange and up towards Hood Hill Plantation.

We walk along the edge of the trees to the track crossing at (11) and here turn left, continuing uphill on the broad forest track into the plantation. Ignoring one wide drive and one grassed-over track on our left, we go as far as the Y-fork at (12). Here we bear left and continue to the road at (13).

Turning left, we use the road up to the Kilburn Woods (White Horse) car park because the footpath shown on the O.S. map is badly overgrown. It's a steep pull up to the car park, but nothing compared to the 151 steps up to the top of the White Horse itself! Never mind; the first class panorama views afford the perfect excuse to stop and catch breath. However at this point we have a dilemma: the official CW route as shown on the O.S. map turns east for some 200m to Low Town Bank Road and so we should really do this short out-and-back extra if we wish to say we've done the whole trail.

From above the White Horse, we continue round the edge of the prehistoric fort site at Roulston Scar and back to Sutton Bank. On this stretch of the walk we have the thrill of dodging glider planes as well as admiring the skills of hang-gliders, para-gliders and microlighters.

Cleveland Circles

Southwoods Hall

Mire Beck

Whitestone Cliff

Garbutt Wood

Gormire Lake

High Cleaves Farm

Hood Grange

Hood Hill Plantation

Roulston Scar

White Horse

Gliding Club

Sutton Bank

Hambleton Down

South Woods

4 hawthorns

A170

from previous walk

Reproduced with kind permission of Ordnance Survey © Crown Copyright NC/04/25461

0   1km
0   0·5 mile

Gliders
Stop Look & Listen

300m
260m
220m
180m
140m
100m

Special Interest – WALK 4

Prehistoric Remains

The Hambleton Hills have numerous prehistoric remains of various ages. The notes below may be used as a summary of some of the features visible on Walk 4 and on subsequent excursions.

Long barrows (long mounds or cairns) date from **Neolithic** times but sadly many have been destroyed. However, about a dozen remain in the region and on Walk 6 we can see the one at Kepwick just west of the Hambleton Street about 300m north of Steeple Cross. This still shows the trenches made by a noted barrow-digger, Canon Greenwell of Durham, in the 19th century. Five skeletons were exhumed when it was excavated.

Perhaps the most interesting barrow, opened up in the 1960s, is the long cairn on Great Ayton Moor (Walk 14). The cairn is unusual as it has a rare stone chamber (5 x 2 m) and a long stone 'tail' comparable to a long barrow. The cairn continued in use in the Bronze Age when cremated human bones and pottery were buried in the adjacent stone circles.

The most detailed investigation (1979-81) of a long barrow was at Street House Farm, Loftus. This is close to Walk 18, although nothing remains visible after the excavation. The barrow had a wooden wall at the east end of the mound with a courtyard beyond. This also continued to be used in the later Bronze Age.

Round barrows (howes or tumuli on O.S. maps) come from the later **Bronze Age** and can be seen on the skyline nearly everywhere across the moors. About 200 barrows have been excavated and recorded, though often they have been mutilated by careless digging methods. Some four-fifths contained Bronze Age pottery and over half had cremated human bones. Only occasionally have more elaborate articles been retrieved. Lines of round barrows run along ridges across the moors and probably formed land boundaries in the Bronze Age, though some were built in large groups as barrow cemeteries.

Cairnfields represent the remains of prehistoric farms and are most easily seen on the spurs of land which project into the dales. There are about 70 on the North York Moors. Cairnfields consist of heaps of stone 5m or less in diameter and scattered in almost random fashion. They are thought to have originated in the Bronze Age but some could be of later date. As soil on farmland became eroded during the Bronze Age, the remaining stones had to be cleared from the fields and these stones were then piled into walls or cairns, the cairns themselves often being stacked up against large earthfast boulders. Cairnfields are found close to Walks 8 and 10.

The Prehistoric Dykes on the North York Moors seem to date from about 1000BC onwards. Cleave Dyke and its connections with the Steeple Cross, Hesketh and Casten Dykes formed a system of territorial boundaries that outlined 'estates' containing all the needs of mixed farming. There was upland grazing, arable land on the lower hills, meadows in the dales and access to river water.

Hill-forts are usually dated from the **Iron Age** though some appear to have been occupied earlier. There are four located around the west and north sides of the moors and three of these sites are passed on Cleveland Circles. All four hill-forts share superb strategic positions along the tops of escarpments overlooking the lowlands beneath. **Roulston Scar** (Walk 4) had a fort with defences around the whole of the White Horse promontory making it the biggest prehistoric enclosure in Yorkshire.

Boltby hill-fort is passed on Walk 5 and **Live Moor fort** on Walk 10 but the fourth fort at **Eston Nab** lies off C.C. routes.

Kilburn's White Horse is the only turf carved figure in northern England but, unlike the chalk-cut figures in southern England, it is cut into gritstone and so after it was first created in 1857 it had to be coated in whitewash. Subsequent maintenance has included the spreading of chalk chippings to cheer up its appearance. The current technique, first tried in 1999, is to use white paint sprayed on with high-powered machinery. But it's likely to be in student Rag Weeks that strips of plastic sheeting change the horse into a highly photogenic zebra!

Garbutt Wood Nature Reserve is nationally important for the range of different rock types exposed in the cliff face and the wood's varied habitats encourage a wide variety of flora.

Lake Gormire is the only natural lake in the N.Y.M.N.P. and was formed when glacial meltwater became trapped between the Vale of York ice-sheet and the Hambleton Hills escarpment.

Hood Castle stood on the top of Hood Hill and was possibly built by Robert de Stuteville before 1135. Its remains are shown on the O.S. map as 'Earthwork'. In 1264 it was given a licence to be fortified and it is last mentioned in 1322 when Edward II took it from Thomas, Earl of Lancaster.

Cooper's Cross has only its base remaining by the side of the A170, about 25m east of the western entrance to the Visitor Centre car park. It stands close to where the Hambleton Drove Road forked east to Malton and south to Oldstead.

Special Interest – WALK 5

The Hillside Parishes are a group of eight parishes along the western side of the Hambleton Hills. Six of the eight churches are visited on C.C. walks and the information below is taken mainly from the churches' very helpful information leaflet.

There has been a church on the site of **St Wilfrid's Church, Kirby Knowle**, for centuries but the present building dates from 1873 and has a tower 'housing three bells and plenty of birds' nests'. The church still uses its 1570 Communion chalice and in the churchyard is a 17th century font.

Holy Trinity Church, Boltby also stands on an old site – a chapel is known to have been founded in 1409. The village was named in the earlier Domesday Survey and the parish registers date back to 1600.

Ravensthorpe (or Boltby) Mill stood on Gurtoft Beck and dates back at least to 1142. Ingenious water storage works ensured a supply of water both to power the corn mill and also to fill the moat surrounding the nearby Ravensthorpe Manor. The mill is now a shell and used as a garage. The old house no longer exists, though the ditch remains, and a newer **Ravensthorpe Manor** was built in the 19th century a little to the west of Boltby.

In the early 19th century, the Boltby Estate was owned by **Edward Manners** who, when he died in 1811, left a highly provocative will. Instead of leaving the 25,000 acre estate to his eldest son, he took the unusual step of splitting the property equally among 10 of his 11 children. Imagine the furore! The settlement was so controversial that the legal disputes between the inheritors went on for 34 years costing, of course, a fortune in legal fees.

In 1859 William Grainge wrote that **linen weaving** was formerly carried on in Boltby 'to a considerable extent'. Unfortunately it is not clear what was meant by a 'considerable extent' though it is thought that the industry was probably not so important as in some of the surrounding villages.

Boltby has an interesting story to tell about its **water supply**. Under an agreement of 1880 village residents were given the perpetual right to free supplies of water for domestic or agricultural use. This arrangement was challenged by Yorkshire Water in the 1980s but the independent Arbitrator judging the case pronounced in 1991 in favour of the villagers and their perpetual right.

Boltby hill-fort was located at Boltby Nab where there is a gap in the Cleave Dyke. Excavation in 1938 found early Bronze Age gold earrings but the fort was destroyed by ploughing in 1961. A fragment of the rampart remains by the path on the scarp top.

Hambleton Hillside Mosaic Walk is a 36-mile circular trail on the edge of the North York Moors. There are 23 different mosaics along this Regional Route. The mosaics were made by local people, both children and adults, and give clues to the special attractions of the area. Some designs show plants and animals while others focus on historical features. The mosaics were fashioned from pieces of broken pottery, tiles, glass and ceramic. To make a mosaic, the design is first prepared face down on a sheet of paper and then concrete is poured on top of it. When the concrete has set the paper is removed and the finished mosaic is revealed. Cleveland Circles pass 10 of the mosaics and 7 of them can be found on Walk 5.

In Boltby, Sarah Tate (aged 13) said she chose a kingfisher for her mosaic 'because my father often sees one on our farm'.

Jessica Tate (aged 8) decided on an Aylesbury duck since this is a popular breed amongst local farmers. 'I chose a dragonfly because in summer they often fly into our conservatory,' explained Hannah Peters (aged 14).

Cross: Kirby Knowle Churchyard has a fine cross by the side of the path but it is not certain whether this is an ancient boundary marker or the remains of a pre-Conquest cross.

WALK 5
near BOLTBY –
STEEPLE CROSS

Map: Explorer OL 26
S.E.P.:   Sneck Yate (509877)
Buses: not available for this walk
Cleveland Way distance: **3.7 miles**
Circular walk distance: **10.1 miles**
Shorter walk alternative: **7.0 miles**
Special interest:
    Kirby Knowle, Boltby, Mosaic Walk
Cross: Kirby Knowle Church (468873)

Although parking is possible in either Kirby Knowle or Boltby, space is limited and so the recommended start is from the small car parking area at Sneck Yate.

We walk down the road from the car park (1) to reach the CW and turn right through attractive woodland. After the wood, the path goes across patchy scrub to the road leading up to High Paradise Farm. Where a track splits off left into Boltby Forest (2), we keep right.

After passing through the farmstead, the CW continues to the Hambleton Road and here we turn left on to the wide grassy drove-road (3). We continue into Boltby Forest and along to the corner of the woodland at (4). On the right of the track through the gate just in front of us is the site of Steeple Cross. However, the present walk turns left before the gate and stays within the forest area perimeter.

Very soon the track splits into three. The shorter walk uses the route on the left and goes through the forest and then via Low Paradise Farm back to Boltby. The longer walk uses the central route.

The central and right-hand paths join together again at (5) and now a little navigational care is needed. We go on for about 80m and here bear left where another path branches off right. After a further 115m or so we go straight ahead at the path crossing and soon a wide sandy bridleway takes us along Windygill Ridge with its fine views over the heather on Cowesby Moor to our right.

When we reach (6), just after a short, slight descent, the path splits. We go right between two birch trees, and stay right, to follow a much narrower bridleway which twists across the moor through heather and scrub birch to the T-junction at (7). Now we leave the moor and go sharp right down the stony track.

Just after bending left, a fingerpost advises us that the p.r.o.w. actually runs parallel to, but slightly to the right of, the wider, drier track. But whichever we use, we are led to a short stretch of grass before reaching the road at Brickshed

Cottage (8). Turning left, we have just under a mile to go along Ingdale Lane to Kirby Knowle.

As we enter the village we come to a T-junction and we note the footpath going straight ahead through a kissing gate. We will soon take this path but first do an out-and-back detour to St Wilfrid's Church along to our right. Returning to the kissing gate, the path goes over two fields to reach the track at the edge of Wind Egg plantation (9). Going straight over the track and up into the wood, we follow signs for Boltby but should be prepared for the path to be muddy after wet weather.

After a 90° left turn at the edge of Storth Wood (10) we continue through the trees still following directions to Boltby. We avoid the private paths to Ravensthorpe Manor before turning 90° right on the bridleway at (11). Then we stay by the edge of two fields (a stile may be missing half-way along) to the corner at (12). Turning left, we carry on to the fingerpost at (13) from where a right turn on the grassy bridleway leads us into Boltby.

We turn left and walk through the settlement, pausing to visit Holy Trinity Church, and continue to the fork at the end of the village. Bearing right at the 'No Through Road' sign we soon cross Lunshaw Beck and then carry on to the end of a wide track at (14). From here we start climbing on a faint path up the open grassy slope towards Cow Pasture Wood.

Veering right where another path branches left, we go for another 100m to the gate into the wood. We remain on the bridleway as we continue to the fingerpost at (15). Here we turn left towards Little Moor and use the sunken track on the left. (Though the O.S. map shows the p.r.o.w. outside the forest, the path on the ground remains at first within the trees.) We leave the trees through a gate to cross a short stretch of open grassy moor before going through another gate. Soon after this we come to a wide forest track (16). We cross straight over, heading up the steep slope into the trees again. The track swings to the right and, just when we start to think 'Are we on the right path?' we reach the gate at the edge of the forest. This will be familiar to those who completed the longer version of Walk 4. A short climb up the now much drier path brings us to the top of the slope (17) and we turn left on to the CW again. There are now a couple of miles of bracing walking along the edge of the escarpment.

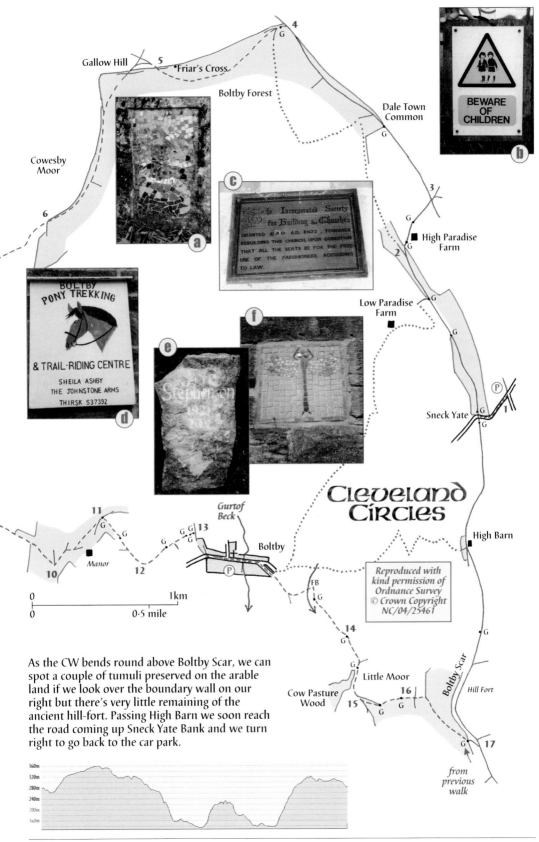

4

G

Gallow Hill 5 •Friar's Cross

Boltby Forest

Dale Town
Common

G

**BEWARE
OF
CHILDREN**

b

Cowesby
Moor

c

3

G

High Paradise
Farm

2 G

6

a

Low Paradise
Farm

G

BOLTBY
PONY TREKKING

& TRAIL·RIDING CENTRE

SHEILA ASHBY
THE JOHNSTONE ARMS
THIRSK 537392

d

f

G

e

P

Sneck Yate G
G

Cleveland
Circles

Gurtof
Beck

11
G   G

G G G 13
G   G

Boltby

High Barn

G

Manor

10   12

P

FB
G

Reproduced with
kind permission of
Ordnance Survey
© Crown Copyright
NC/04/25461

G

0   1km
├────────────┤
0   0·5 mile

14
G

G

As the CW bends round above Boltby Scar, we can
spot a couple of tumuli preserved on the arable
land if we look over the boundary wall on our
right but there's very little remaining of the
ancient hill-fort. Passing High Barn we soon reach
the road coming up Sneck Yate Bank and we turn
right to go back to the car park.

Little Moor

Cow Pasture
Wood   15

16
G

Boltby Scar

Hill Fort

G   17

from
previous
walk

360m
320m
280m
240m
200m
160m

WALK 6
STEEPLE CROSS –
DUNSFORTH'S HILL

Map: Explorer OL 26
S.E.P.: Kepwick (468909)
Buses: not available for this walk
Cleveland Way distance: **1.3 miles**
Circular walk distance: **12.1 miles**
Shorter walk alternatives:
      West Loop   **7.2 miles**
      East Loop   **5.0 miles**
Special interest:
    Steeple Cross, Friar's Cross, Arden Hall
Crosses: Friar's Cross (488899) Steeple Cross
    (495902) Kepwick Cross (468917)

We park either at Kepwick village car park or the road-end on the Cleveland Way. (The latter start allows a figure of eight to be completed if there are two groups wishing to do different length walks but don't try getting up there in snow!)

From the Kepwick car park we walk out of the village, past the church and turn left on the path opposite Monument View (1). This leads us up past the Obelisk war memorial on our right and we follow the waymarked path around field edges and over stiles to Cowesby Church.

We continue from the church through the village and take the track shown as 'No Through Road' up into the trees and then fork right at (2). When the trees on our right end, we need to branch left upslope on the 'Footpath to Helmsley'. This zigzags up to the edge of the moorland (3) where we turn right and follow the bridleway. We first cross a short stretch of open moor but soon come to a gate and then go along the right-hand side of the stone wall. Rising gently, we bend round Gallow Hill and reach Boltby Forest (4).

In contrast to the last walk, we use the path just inside the boundary wall, rather than the bridleway, walking past Friar's Cross and up to the CW (5). Directly ahead of us lie the remains of the shaft of Steeple Cross.

We turn left and follow the broad Hambleton Drove Road. A Neolithic long barrow, rare in this area, as well as several tumuli are located on our left by a trig point. Passing the road-end car parking spot at (6) we continue to the path crossing at (7). Older maps show this as the site of Limekiln House, a former drovers' inn which was also linked with the limestone industry. Those opting for the shorter walk here go left through the gate back to Kepwick; the longer walk goes right on the grassy bridleway over the

hummocks of the disused quarry. After 100m or so we need to fork left to the waymarked gate and then walk on the left side of the fence over the heather and bracken. A steep descent takes us into Thorodale and then by the ford shown on the O.S. map at (8) we keep left, leave the stream and go up towards the wood. Entering the trees, we follow the p.r.o.w. for a little over a mile on a fine woodland path through mixed conifers and deciduous trees to the path junction at (9). Bending back right on ourselves, the track leads over a small stream and round left to the front of Arden Hall.

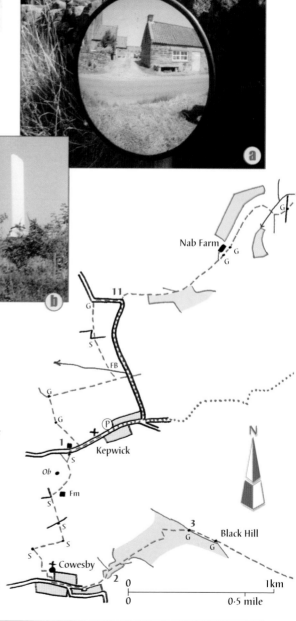

Turning right when we are at the Hall, we soon turn right again (10) and follow the wide track signposted to Kepwick. At first this goes through more pleasant woodland but then leaves the trees and crosses over open moorland; it can feel a bit exposed in the wind but there are good views on both sides.

When we reach the Cleveland Way again (6), we have a choice. We can use the road directly ahead of us to return to Kepwick (this will save a duplication of route next time) or if we wish to avoid the tarmac, we retrace our earlier steps northwards to the site of Limekiln House at (7) and take the path through the gate on our left. This is the route of the short walk - it's a delightful path leading down to Kepwick. At first we keep to the wall on our left and avoid a couple of small paths leading off right to an old quarry. Then the path leaves the wall, crosses a small stream, passes on the left side of Nab Farm and comes to the road at Cross Lodge (11).

An easy option here is to turn left and use the road back to Kepwick but a more interesting way is to turn right and go to the road bend about 200m away. The fingerpost directs us left over arable land to a stile half-hidden in the field corner and from there we cross another field to Bridge Beck. Crossing the stream, we need to bear left towards a gap in the hedge alongside the old dismantled tramway that used to be used for transporting limestone from Kepwick quarry. On the tramway we turn right for about 400m or so to a p.r.o.w. crossing our route. We turn left and cross two fields as we rise gently up towards Kepwick village. Reaching the road, we go left to the Church and back to our starting point.

Special Interest notes for WALK 6 appear on page 30

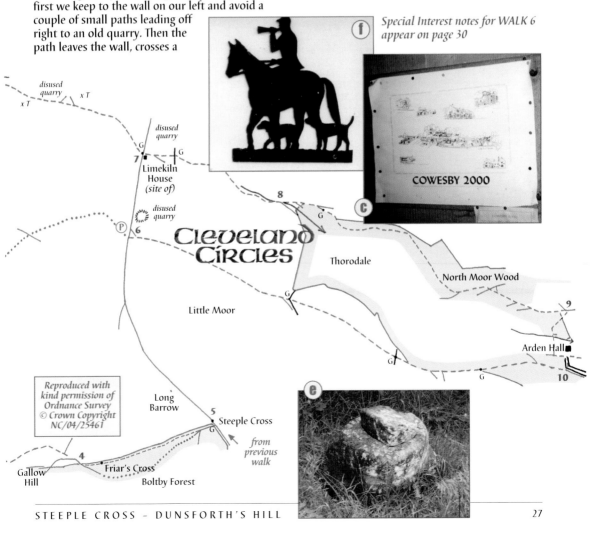

disused quarry
x T   x T

disused quarry

7 G
Limekiln House (site of)
G

disused quarry
P 6

8
G

COWESBY 2000

Cleveland Circles

Thorodale

North Moor Wood

Little Moor
G

9

Arden Hall
G
10

Long Barrow
5
Steeple Cross
G

from previous walk

4
Gallow Hill
Friar's Cross
Boltby Forest

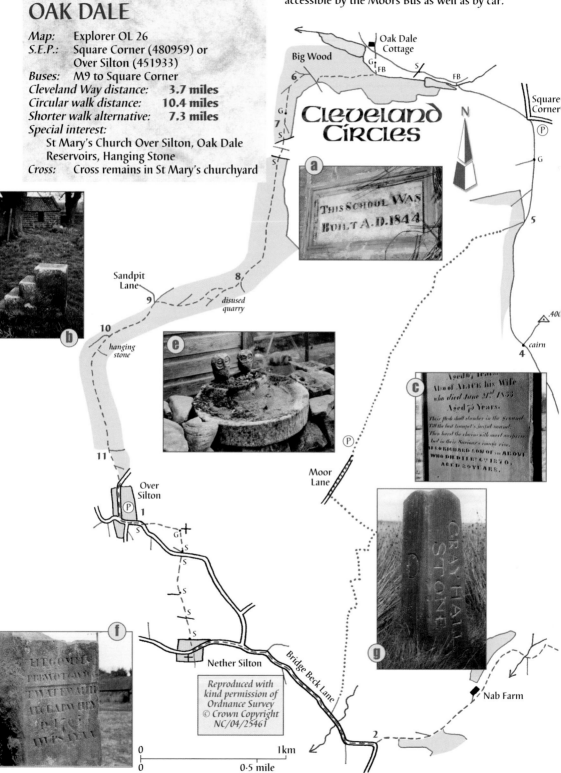

WALK 7
DUNSFORTH'S HILL –
OAK DALE

We may wish to start this walk from either Over Silton or Nether Silton. Alternatively, we can begin from the car park at Square Corner which is accessible by the Moors Bus as well as by car.

Map: Explorer OL 26
S.E.P.: Square Corner (480959) or Over Silton (451933)
Buses: M9 to Square Corner
Cleveland Way distance: **3.7 miles**
Circular walk distance: **10.4 miles**
Shorter walk alternative: **7.3 miles**
Special interest:
   St Mary's Church Over Silton, Oak Dale Reservoirs, Hanging Stone
Cross: Cross remains in St Mary's churchyard

Big Wood

Oak Dale Cottage

Square Corner

Cleveland Circles

a THIS SCHOOL WAS BUILT A.D. 1844

Sandpit Lane

disused quarry

400

cairn

e

hanging stone

b

c

Over Silton

Moor Lane

g CRAY HALL STONE

Nab Farm

f

Nether Silton

Bridge Beck Lane

Reproduced with kind permission of Ordnance Survey © Crown Copyright NC/04/25461

0 ————— 1km
0 ————— 0·5 mile

However, this means we split the Cleveland Way section into two parts, one at the beginning and one at the end of the walk. The shorter walk, which does not visit the villages, begins at the F.C. picnic site on Moor Lane and crosses farmland to Bridge Beck Lane.

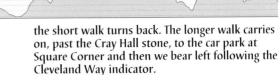

Assuming we are starting from Over Silton, we walk south through the village, bend left and continue to the road corner at (1). Here an indicator post directs us over a stile and we continue to the delightful Norman church of St Mary Magdalene; it's not visible until the last minute because it is hidden from the rest of the village behind a small rise in the land.

Leaving the church we walk due south and negotiate five stiles to Nether Silton. We should make sure to go directly across the road and through the gate to look at the tall stone standing in the field a little way ahead to our right. Returning to the road, we turn left to visit All Saints Church and then right to walk roughly eastwards along Bridge Beck Lane and over Sorrow Beck as far as the road bend at (2). This is the point we came to on the previous walk and from here we re-trace our steps, but in the opposite direction to last time, through Nab Farm and back up the steep hillside to the Cleveland Way at (3).

At this point we turn left and follow the National Trail along Hambleton Street for about two miles round the top end of White Gill to the large cairn at (4). This marks the end of the short path that leads off right to the trig point (399m) on Black Hambleton. (Interestingly for those of a peak-bagging frame of mind, the O.S. shows a spot height of exactly 400m just slightly to the NE of the trig point. But it's in the middle of the heather!)

Continuing on the main Cleveland Way track, the surface is a little uneven underfoot as we drop down from Black Hambleton and move off the limestone on to sandstone, grits and shales. We soon come to the signpost on our left at (5) directing us through the forest to Nether Silton. This is where the short walk turns back. The longer walk carries on, past the Cray Hall stone, to the car park at Square Corner and then we bear left following the Cleveland Way indicator.

Taking the stepped path down the slope we should be on the lookout for red-legged partridge that inhabit this part of the bracken-covered moorland. We cross the footbridge over Jenny Brewster's Gill and then go by the side of Oakdale Upper Reservoir but beware – this place is the home of backcasting anglers!

About 300m or so after the reservoir dam, we approach Oak Dale Cottage. Here we need to be careful. At the cottage we turn back sharp left on ourselves and go down to the waymarked gate that then leads us into the trees and along to a footbridge. There is now a steep pull up through the birch trees, bluebells, rhododendrons and bracken but the p.r.o.w. is clearly marked. At the top of the slope, we turn right along the flat for 100m before bending left at the waymark (6).

We now follow the contour through Big Wood and round the edge of Thimbleby Moor on a delightful path with seemingly masses of bilberry plants. We pass through a pheasant protection gate and then at (7) we need to do a right-left shimmy before carrying on to a stile, across a stony track and then into the trees again, as far as the huge pillar of rock at (8).

From here the path goes down for about 80 paces and then the p.r.o.w. bears off right continuing down the hillside. (It's easy to continue straight ahead on the clearer path but if we do this, we can take another narrow path on the right about 200m further on.) Whichever line we use, it's a lovely, though sometimes muddy, stretch down through Thimbleby Bank Plantation until we reach the bridleway at (9).

Now we turn left, continue through the wood and take the left branching bridleway at (10). Shortly after the track swings left, we should make a slight detour left up the hillside on a faint path to the Hanging Stone with its superb views over The Vale of Mowbray. Where this steep path curls right, the viewpoint is immediately on our left.

Returning down to the bridleway, the main track soon bends left again, rises gently and then at (11) turns abruptly left. Here we take the narrow path off right by an isolated gatepost. Following this, we're soon back in Over Silton and turn right towards the houses.

Map labels: Black Hambleton • Hambleton Street • Kepwick Moor • disused quarry • disused quarry • 3 • from previous walk

Special Interest – WALK 6

Arden Hall is described by Pevsner as 'a perfect Queen Anne stone house in a perfect sheltered position'. The house stands on the site of a Benedictine nunnery of which the only remains is a wide chimneybreast inside the building.

The **Memorial Chapel, Kepwick** was built in 1894. Originally it was a Mission Room but it was rebuilt and expanded by the Warner family whose only son was shot down in World War I. We pass the Warner Memorial obelisk on Walk 6. The private chapel now belongs to the Guthe family.

St Michael and All Angels Church, Cowesby occupies the site of a Saxon church and, although the present building was erected in 1846, records go back as far as 1679 and the church contains some attractive Jacobean woodwork. Inside the porch is picture commemorating life in Cowesby in 2000.

WARNING
FISHERMEN BACKCASTING
Please
STAY ON THE FOOTPATH

Friar's Cross: The base of this cross can be found at the edge of the forest adjacent to the old track known as 'Red Gate' which runs from Steeple Cross to the tumulus on Gallow Howe. The cross would once have been on the open moorland of Boltby Moor.

Steeple Cross: 'Stepicros' is named in a legal document of 1246 which mentions the 'King's Road', namely, Hambleton Street. There is no longer any sign of the wheelhead cross which at one time accompanied the boulder we see today. Steeple Cross and Friar's Cross both stand on the line of the Steeple Dyke.

Kepwick Cross: Some maps show a cross in a field adjoining Cross Lodge. The simple base has been moved so that it is now behind the building.

Special Interest – WALK 7

St Mary's Church, Over Silton, lies separated from its village and it is unclear what happened to the original settlement. The church has an impressive 12th century Norman arch over the main door and a font of the same or earlier age. The roof beams came from old ships' timbers at Hartlepool. As we enter the churchyard, we note the facilities provided for a visiting priest: a stable for his horse to the left of the gate and a mounting block on the right. Unusual rectangular tombstones date from the 18th century, though some modern ones have copied the style.

All Saints Church, Nether Silton, is much newer than St Mary's, having been rebuilt in 1812 but the font is of Norman age. The church altar rails are made from wood taken from HMS Dreadnought, the naval training ship of Nelson's day. In the field to the south of the church stands a mysterious stone with a coded message. Each of the letters carved on the stone is supposed to represent the initial letter of a word that makes up the following message:

*'Here The Grand Old Manor House Stood
The Black Beams Were Oak The Great Walls Were Good
The Walls At The East Wing Are Hidden Here
A Thatched Cottage Like A Barn Was Here Erected Year A.D. 1765
A Wide Porch Spans A Yard And Alcove'*

This memorial was allegedly the idea of Squire Hicks who in the 18th century wanted to mark the site of the former medieval manor house.

Cross: Cross remains among the tombstones in St Mary's churchyard.

Cray Hall boundary stone. According to the National Park's gazetteer, no such place as Cray Hall exists.

Mount Grace Priory
WALK 8

Mount Grace Priory has the most complete remains of any of the nine Carthusian monasteries in England. The Carthusian Order was founded at La Chartreuse in 1084 and the first monastery in England was set up in 1178 at Witham in Somerset by Henry II as part of his penance for the murder of Thomas Becket in Canterbury Cathedral in 1170. The Mount Grace Priory was the eighth English Carthusian settlement (or 'Charterhouse') and was established in 1398.

Mount Grace Priory

The Carthusian monks, like the Cistercians, wore white habits and sought seclusion from the wider world. Each monk had his own two-storey cell where he worked, ate and slept and each cell, with its own garden, was completely cut off from its neighbours. Water was channelled to the cells through pipes from the monastery's own spring. The upper storeys of the cells are thought to have been workshops where the monks, in the days before printing presses, would copy old books and manuscripts. There were 24 cells at Mount Grace and one of these has been reconstructed to show its original form.

The monks' solitary and austere life made them almost like hermits. They ate separately except on Sundays and on special feast days. Food was brought to them in their cells and delivered through a special hatch that was designed so that the monks could not see the person who was serving them. Lay brothers did the kitchen work as well as tending the barns, stables and guesthouse.

Carthusian Monks were not allowed to speak with each other except for a short time on Sunday afternoons and when they walked outside the monastery once a week. There was no hospital or infirmary because when a monk became ill he was cared for in his own cell.

When Mount Grace surrendered in 1539 to Henry VIII's Dissolution of the Monasteries, it suffered less than some of the other Carthusian Charterhouses. Three of their nine Priors were executed for refusing to accept the King's demands and at the London house one third of the monks suffered the same fate.

Mount Grace does not possess the magnificent architecture of either Rievaulx or Byland Abbey. The individual lifestyle of a relatively small number of brothers meant there was less need for a large church or chapter house and the general lack of communal living removed the need for a large refectory and dormitory. Perhaps the simplicity of Mount Grace, rather than the grandeur of the Cistercian Houses, gives a more accurate picture of the original strict and austere life that the Rule of St Benedict was designed to inculcate amongst the Orders of White Monks.

WALK 8
OAK DALE –
SOUTH WOOD

Map: Explorer OL 26
S.E.P.:   Cod Beck Reservoir (Sheepwash) car
            park (468993). Toilets in Osmotherley
Buses: 80, 89 to Osmotherley
Cleveland Way distance: **2.6 miles**
Circular walk distance: **9.2 miles**
      (incl out-and-back to Mount Grace Priory)
Shorter walk alternatives:
    North loop (from Sheepwash)
                         6.1 miles
    South loop (from Osmotherley)
                         4.3 miles
Special interest:
    Mount Grace Priory, Lady Chapel,
    Osmotherley
Crosses: Osmotherley Market Cross (456972)
    and shaft of old cross

This walk has numerous possible variations with a choice of starting points but the CW section runs from Oak Dale Farm through Osmotherley and up to South Wood. One possibility is to do a figure of eight walk centred on Osmotherley. The National Trust kindly allows parking at the Sheepwash car park and the Forestry Commission permits walking on their paths through Cod Beck Woods. However, these concessions do not in any way indicate any general right of public access.

We shall assume that we are starting from Cod Beck Reservoir (Sheepwash) car park and picnic site – families with small children may wish to do a circuit of the reservoir and then spend time playing in the stream by the picnic site.

From the car park we cross the stream and take the path along the SE side of the reservoir. When we reach the dam we turn left and use the concessionary track through the wood. We may want to follow this as far as High Lane, but a more pleasant route branches off quickly right on a narrow path through an avenue of cypress trees (1). Then at the p.r.o.w. crossing (2) we turn left and take a fine trail through old, mature woodland.

At High Lane (3) we turn right and join the old Hambleton Drove Road. The track shortly becomes surfaced and takes us past the site of **Solomon's Temple**. An old hermit, Matt Walker, planned to spend his latter years here but ran out of money for completing the building of his retirement home. He long held squatter's possession rights over the site. A little further on we come to **Chequers**, an old drove road inn. This was one of several inns that claimed that their turf fire had been kept alight for over 200 years. Shortly after this (4), we leave the road, taking the path on our right and making our way to Oak Dale. A quick glance at the O.S. map might surprise us as we learn that Middlesbrough lies just 300m to our left.

At Oak Dale we join the Cleveland Way and turn right, go through the trees and cross Slape Stones Beck as it flows into the lower reservoir. When we reach the road (5) we do a quick left-right manoeuvre and continue upslope on the CW before branching off left towards Whitehouse Farm. A minor re-alignment of the route avoids the farm buildings and takes us down to the footbridge over Cod Beck. Steps then lead up through the wood and when we emerge we follow the waymarks sending us left into Osmotherley.

Going through a narrow snicket and passing the Methodist Chapel, we come to the village square. There should be time to turn left and visit the Anglican Church before continuing on the CW up the hill, calling at the Roman Catholic Monastery on the way. At Ruebury Lane (6) the CW and the longer walk turn left whilst the shorter walk continues on Quarry Lane before turning right towards the Cote Ghyll caravan site.

When we swing round at the viewpoint (7), we need to take the path on our right up to the Mount Grace Lady Chapel and when we have visited there we can use the concessionary path that comes back from the northern end of the Chapel precinct to Chapel Wood Farm (8). If we wish to visit Mount Grace Priory itself, we now have an out-and-back walk from the farm to the priory. At first we cross a small field, then follow the hedge before entering Mount Grace Wood for a delightful

stroll down to the Priory. But we should remember that it's a bit of a climb back up to the farm!

We continue northwards on the CW and when we enter the trees at (9) take the way-marked right fork. After climbing steadily for about 500m to the end of

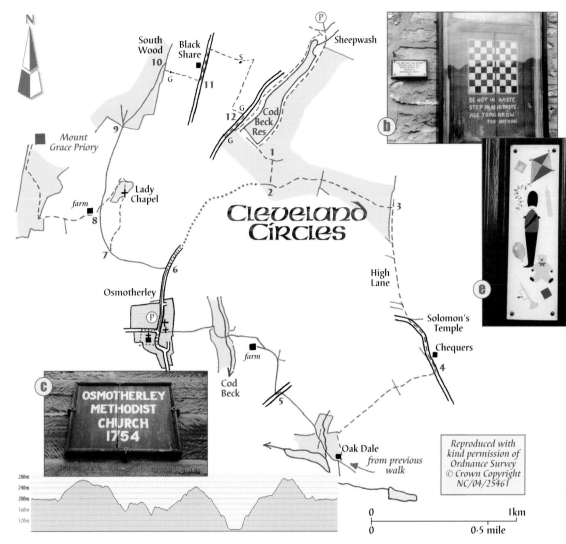

N

South Wood
10

Black Share
11

S

G

9

Mount Grace Priory

Sheepwash

P

12

G

Cod Beck Res

G

1

farm

Lady Chapel

8

2

3

Cleveland Circles

7

6

High Lane

Osmotherley

P

Solomon's Temple

Chequers
4

farm

Cod Beck

5

Oak Dale

from previous walk

280m
240m
200m
160m
120m

0   1km
0   0·5 mile

the conifers, the main track turns sharp right (10). Here we take the narrow path immediately on our right. It's just by some gorse bushes and we more or less turn back on ourselves. But it's easy to miss, so be watchful. We walk through bracken and bilberry, pass through the gate in the wall and then follow the field boundary to the road at (11).

Now we turn left, go past Black Share farm buildings and turn right at the fingerpost. We follow the field edge, cross a stile and then about 40m further on the path turns down left through bracken scrub. Soon we swing right and, catching views of Cod Beck Reservoir down to our left, continue past more gorse until we reach a stone wall. Here we turn left down to the road (12).

We turn right and need to walk past the dam in order to reach the gate which allows us access to the path that takes us back along the NW side of the reservoir to our start.

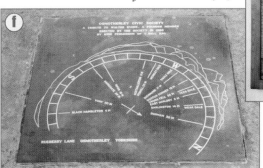

Special Interest – WALK 8

Osmotherley Walkers – beware of Osmotherley! It's the sort of delightful spot where intrepid ramblers are suddenly beguiled into idle dawdling as they explore its fascinating layout and history. The village used to provide accommodation for workers in the nearby alum quarries and jet mines and it was a centre for the linen weaving industry based on water power from Cod Beck. The Youth Hostel at Cote Ghyll is a former mill which finally closed in 1915.

Osmotherley's four churches and chapels are all of interest. **St Peter's Anglican Church** is a 12th century church which was largely rebuilt following its destruction by the Scots in 1322. Stones with Anglo-Danish carvings are on display in the fine 15th century porch. John Wesley preached on numerous occasions in Osmotherley; sometimes supposedly from the butter table; and a few years after his first visit in 1745 the **Methodist Chapel** in Chapel Passage was built.

As we walk along North End through the village, we pass on our right the Monastery Church, a building which acts as both Roman Catholic Church and also as monastery for a small community of Benedictine monks. This chapel dates from around the 16th century when it was dangerous to be a Roman Catholic and this helps explain why the building is disguised to look like an ordinary house. It was given to the Franciscan friars in 1665 so that they could minister to pilgrims making their way to the Mount Grace Lady Chapel outside the village. Since 1994 Benedictine monks from Ampleforth Abbey have used the building as their monastery. Relations between the different Christian denominations in the village are good and it is interesting to note that John Wesley was first invited to the village by the Franciscan priest and Wesley preached first in the Franciscan chapel.

The origins of the **Mount Grace Lady Chapel** are obscure but a licence for Mass to be said here was granted in 1397 which implies that the chapel existed before that date. Over time the chapel fell into disrepair and then in 1942 two priests who were cycling in the area came across the overgrown ruins. A campaign began to restore the Lady Chapel and the new building was opened in 1961. Further improvements have since been made and the chapel, in the care of Benedictine monks from Ampleforth, is used by pilgrims from different Christian communities.

Osmotherley's **Market Cross** stands in the centre of the village next to a stone slab table that has been known both as the 'butter table' since butter was sold from it and the 'coffin table' because coffins were rested on it during funerals. The present cross is a 19th century replacement mounted on the 14th century base. Part of the original cross shaft now stands next door to 12 West End.

Special Interest – WALK 9

Whorlton is described by Nikolaus Pevsner as 'an eerie place, with a church in ruins, a castle in ruins, and hardly anything else' - to a romantic, this might be taken as a compliment! The castle, known as Potto in 1216, was a motte and bailey structure with a wide ditch but a report of 1343 described the castle as ruinous. So what we see today, the oblong gatehouse and the tunnel-vaulted cellars, are the remains of the castle built later in the fourteenth century by the de Meynells. Above the gateway are the arms of the Meynell, Greystock and d'Arcy families, with Meynell impaling Darcy. The extensive earthworks around the castle site show that there was formerly a sizeable medieval settlement here, reduced perhaps by the plague.

Holy Cross (Old) Church at Whorlton was built in the Norman period but is redundant and because of its derelict condition is only occasionally used for services. However, it is possible to peer through the door to view the bog oak effigy commemorating the second Lord Nicholas de Meynell who died in 1322. Bog oak is oak embedded in bogs and preserved from decay. Holy Cross (New) Church in Swainby acts as the replacement for the old church.

Whorl Hill, an outlier separated from the main escarpment of the Cleveland Hills, was the site of a valuable find of Roman silver coins hidden in a large silver vase and discovered by a farmer as he was ploughing his fields in 1810.

Stone: A memorial stone to Bill Cowley stands beside the Cleveland Way in Clain Wood. Bill Cowley pioneered the Lyke Wake Walk across the North York Moors in 1955.

Special Interest – WALK 10

Lord Stones Café is located by the site of an ancient monument comprising two mounds which are round barrows, 15m and 12.5m in diameter. A number of large stones surround the southern barrow and one of these stones, known as the Three Lords' Stone, has some prehistoric cup marks engraved into it. This particular stone was used as the boundary stone marking the intersection of the three old estates of Helmsley, Whorlton and Busby.

Raisdale Mill seems relatively isolated but it is believed to have been the mill for a lost settlement sited near Hall Garth Farm. It is mentioned in a document of 1539 and was rebuilt in 1849. Operations ceased around 1910 and the building was converted into a house in the 1980s.

Scugdale's pretty appearance today belies the history of its former mining activities. In 1857 the opening of a short stretch of rail line allowed the development of **ironstone mining** to take place on a commercial scale and mines were opened at Coalmire and above Huthwaite Green. However, the venture was troubled with flooding problems as well as foreign competition and the mines closed thirty years later. As iron-working declined, many of the miners turned their experience instead to **jet mining** but this industry, too, had a limited life and had finished by 1892.

Jet consists of fossilised wood that was a variety of Araucaria similar to, though much bigger than, today's 'monkey puzzle' tree. It looks like coal in appearance and the tough 'hard jet' of N.E. Yorkshire and Cleveland is the type most easily polished into ornaments. The jet is found randomly in shale rocks that may be up to 10m thick lying above the ironstone strata and below the alum shales.

During the 19th century jet was mined in numerous locations along the coast and on moorland valley sides. Adits (or parallel drifts) were dug into the hillsides for a maximum of about 100m. A special pick with which to work the shales was the jet miner's main tool; explosives were not used as these were more likely to have broken the jet deposits.

Jet objects have been found in prehistoric graves 4,000 years old and there are references to jet working at Whitby in 1394. However, it was the impetus given by Queen Victoria following the death of Prince Albert in 1861 that led to the great increase in popularity of black jet jewellery and the peaking of the industry in the 1870s. Most of the jet was sent to Whitby where at the height of the industry there were over 200 workshops processing jet into ornaments and the workshop operating today at the top of Church Street shows the different stages involved in changing rock into jewellery. But the boom did not last long and Whitby's workshops suffered in the face of cheap imports of 'soft jet' from Spain as well as imitation jet from France.

Clear evidence of jet mining is visible along the valley sides of Scugdale and Bilsdale (Walk 11) as well as along the escarpment between Osmotherley and Guisborough. Abandoned adits and long lines of waste tips mark the sites of the former mines. Subsidence of the land above the shallow drifts has sometimes caused problems when farmers have suddenly lost machinery or animals down a hole in the ground.

The jet shales contain oil and sometimes the tips were deliberately set on fire in order to produce a hardened material that could be used for improving track surfaces. This burning explains the presence of the bright red waste piles we see in some places today.

The **Giant of Scugdale**, Harry Cooper, lived for part of his life at Scugdale Hall. At eight feet six inches (260 cm) he was alleged to be the tallest man in the world when he was exhibited in the U.S.A. in the nineteenth century. When he died, aged 41, he weighed 29 stones (185 kg).

Live Moor hill-fort was discovered relatively recently, even though the Lyke Wake Walk cuts through its eastern rampart. An old trackway connects the fort to the cairnfield on the moor top, suggesting a likely Bronze Age date.

Donna Cross is easy to find. It lies immediately to the right of the CW path about 100m before the track intersection at (3). The base stone is a boulder with a socket carved into it and the cross is mentioned in 1637 as a 'shaft in socket boundary marker'. The E on the north side of the stone stands for the Emmerson family of Easby and the F on the south side for the Fevershams of Helmsley. A short way to the north of the cross is an 18th century boundary stone with NORTH engraved on what is almost the east side of the stone.

Peacock at Raisdale Mill. These resplendent creatures can also be seen (and heard) on Walk 24 and Walk 11 (short circuit).

WALK 9
SOUTH WOOD –
LIVE MOOR

Map: Explorer OL 26
S.E.P.T.: Swainby (476022)
Buses: 80, 89, M9
Cleveland Way distance: **3.8 miles**
Circular walk distance: **10.2 miles**
Shorter walk alternatives:
    West loop   **6.6 miles**
    East loop   **5.3 miles**
Special interest:
    Whorlton Church and Castle remains
Cross or Stone:
    Memorial stone to Bill Cowley (478005)

This walk includes visits to Faceby and Swainby as well as to the remains of Whorlton's Church and Castle. The longer route splits easily into two sections if we use the Coalmire Lane link back to Swainby.

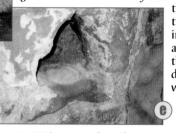

We start walking from Swainby where there are three pubs as well as public toilets. Parking should be possible along the roadside next to the stream running through the village centre.

From the Church of the Holy Cross we walk SE down the main street to the Miners Arms pub and here turn right into Claver Close to pick up the p.r.o.w. between the houses at the far end of the Close. This field-side path leads us to Back Lane (1) where we turn left.

At the second road bend (2) we fork right on to the bridleway which takes us past Scarth Lees to Scarth Wood Farm where we go between the buildings and then turn sharp right along the grassy track between hedge and fence.

Walking along the edge of Arncliffe Wood and avoiding a bridleway going off to our right (3), we continue on the wide F.C. track round to the intersection at (4). Here we turn right and carry on to the drive leading down right to Arncliffe Hall and Church. We may do a short out-and-back investigation if we wish and then we continue up into the Cleveland Forest. We are now following

the Coast to Coast route. This certainly makes for easy navigation and, after we turn right from the forest track on to the p.r.o.w. at (5), we continue climbing up the slope before turning sharp left as we join the Cleveland Way. From here we now follow the National Trail for nearly four miles.

The first few hundred metres retrace the route we used on Walk 8 but this time when we reach the turn-off to Black Share Farm, we stay on the CW and continue past the BT and TV relay station to the major path junction at (6). To our right is the LWW path coming up from Sheepwash car park but we follow the most obvious track as it goes over Scarth Wood Moor and down to the road at Scarth Nick (7), a glacial overflow channel and part of the old Drove Road.

A left turn to the cattle grid brings us to the gate allowing entry to Coalmire Wood and then there is easy walking to the fork at (8). The Cleveland Way goes left down the long stepped slope and then at the path crossing (9) the shorter walk goes left on the bridleway back to Swainby but the longer route turns left and then immediately right as it continues through more delightful woodland.

At (10) we use the stile to take us over pasture and down to the road where we turn left, cross the fords over Piper Beck and Scugdale Beck and then continue up to the road junction and phone box at (11). Our route crosses the road and follows the edge of the trees to the path fork at (12). Here we leave the CW and

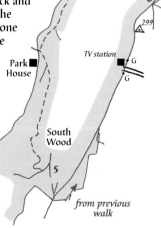

Arncliffe Wood

3

Arncliffe   Hall

4

6

299

TV station

Park House

South Wood

5

from previous walk

300m
260m
220m
180m
140m
120m

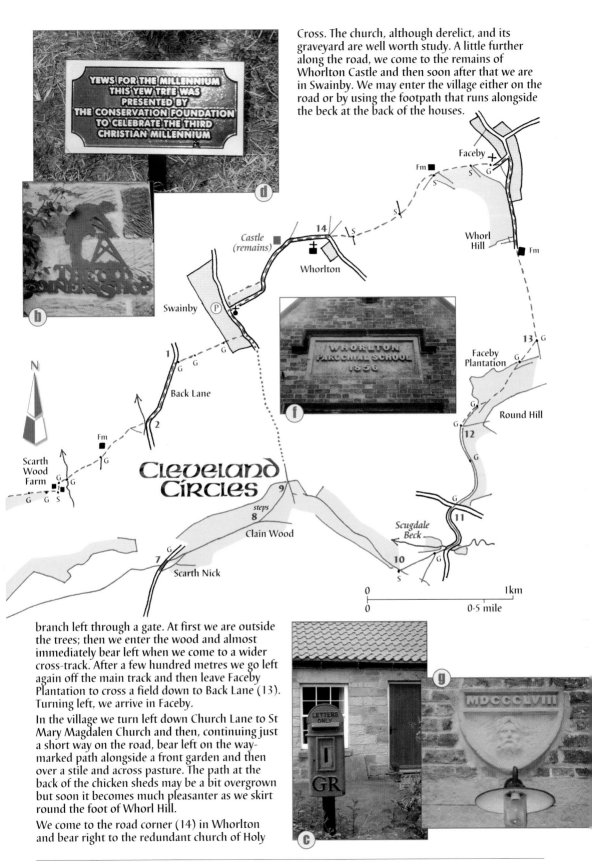

Cross. The church, although derelict, and its graveyard are well worth study. A little further along the road, we come to the remains of Whorlton Castle and then soon after that we are in Swainby. We may enter the village either on the road or by using the footpath that runs alongside the beck at the back of the houses.

branch left through a gate. At first we are outside the trees; then we enter the wood and almost immediately bear left when we come to a wider cross-track. After a few hundred metres we go left again off the main track and then leave Faceby Plantation to cross a field down to Back Lane (13). Turning left, we arrive in Faceby.

In the village we turn left down Church Lane to St Mary Magdalen Church and then, continuing just a short way on the road, bear left on the way-marked path alongside a front garden and then over a stile and across pasture. The path at the back of the chicken sheds may be a bit overgrown but soon it becomes much pleasanter as we skirt round the foot of Whorl Hill.

We come to the road corner (14) in Whorlton and bear right to the redundant church of Holy

WALK 10
LIVE MOOR –
COLD MOOR

Map: Explorer OL 26
S.E.P.: Huthwaite Green (492007)
Toilets at Lord Stones Café
Bus: M9 to Lord Stones Café
Cleveland Way distance: **4.2 miles**
Circular walk distance: **10.0 miles**
Shorter walk alternatives:
West loop **6.6 miles**
East loop **6.8 miles**
Special interest:
Three Lords' Stone, Raisdale Mill, Scugdale
Cross: Donna Cross (545034)

This walk includes some of the most spectacular scenery along the CW as well as some much less frequented tracks. There are four hills to be negotiated – one of them is very steep and those doing the longer circuit may have one place where basic compass navigational skill will be useful. Two moderate length circuits are possible if we use the bridleway between Lord Stones Café and Scugdale Hall.

Parking is best at Lord Stones Café but this will necessitate breaking the CW section of the walk in

two and so for the purposes of this route description it is assumed that we start at the cluster of houses just east of Huthwaite Green where there is enough room for about four cars.

For the first 500m or so we follow the part of the CW covered on Walk 9 but this time when we reach the path fork at (1) we follow the acorn and bear right uphill through the trees. The way has been stone-pitched and paved for much of today's CW stretch and so there is no navigation difficulty ... it's just the inclines that may cause problems! In late summer the heather gives off its gorgeous sweet scent as we climb Round Hill, cross Live Moor with its prehistoric cairnfield, and then go up Gold Hill.

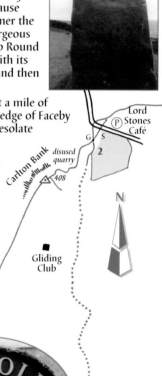

After that there's about a mile of steady climb along the edge of Faceby Bank, past the rather desolate runway tracks of the Carlton Moor Gliding Club and on to the trig point above Carlton

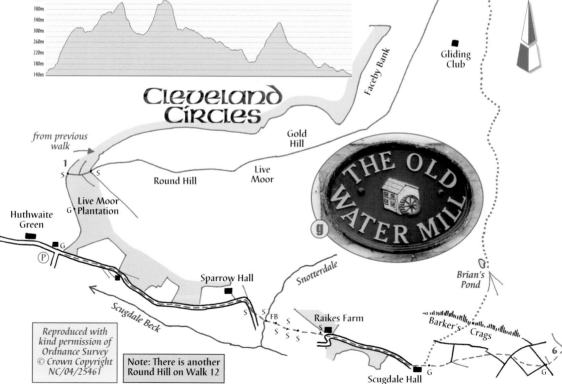

Note: There is another Round Hill on Walk 12

Bank. Views from here, as from other points along the route, arouse all the usual hyperboles.

A steep descent, along which we are warned to avoid the dangerous old mineworking area on our left, brings us down to a bridleway. Here the shorter walk turns right and goes across Whorlton Moor into Scugdale. The longer circuit continues straight ahead on the flagged path, crosses the road close to two ancient tumuli and then takes the path round to the left of the Lord Stones Café. Here there are refreshments and toilets as well as a display of Bronze Age flints found on the site.

The CW leads off behind the clump of trees planted in memory of Alan & Annie Falconer and then goes more or less straight up Cringle Moor. On clear days, the viewfinder at the top of the hill allows a fine excuse to stop and survey the huge sweep of

countryside in front of us. Continuing round the edge of Cringle Moor/Kirby Bank we pass the Bronze Age tumulus of Drake Howe to our right and then soon drop steeply to the track junction at (3), keeping alert in order to spot Donna Cross by the side of the track. We use the CW indicators directing us right through a gate for 50m and then left, but instead of continuing up the hill, we turn right again and continue due south following the fingerpost to Beak Hills.

From Beak Hills Farm the route is tarred and after another mile and a half, just before Stone Intake Farm, we must look for the waymarked stile in the hedge on our right (4). Markers lead us over two fields to a minor road where we go right and then come to the road bend at (5).

We need to be careful here. Turning left to the Raisdale Mill House Holiday Cottages (listen for the peacock), we come to a cluster of buildings and, ignoring the p.r.o.w. going straight ahead, turn sharp left through the central courtyard area. Immediately after the last building, we turn right off the main concrete drive and follow the sign for Mill Lane; it doesn't look like a 'lane' but is more akin to a sunken path. Tree-lined at first, Mill Lane soon opens out and we walk along a wide bridleway track with a stone wall on our left.

Where the overhead electricity wires cross the track intersection at the top of the hill slope (6), we must exercise caution because the path on the ground is slightly different from the p.r.o.w. shown on the O.S. map. The main stony track curves left but we leave this track and bear slightly right towards the waymarked electricity pole and then a fingerpost. However we ignore the fingerpost and instead carry straight on down to the 'Shut this gate' opening. From here the path is clear as we descend into the valley of Scugdale.

Joining a wider track, we bend right to Scugdale Hall (home of the former Scugdale Giant) where the shorter walk joins in and we then continue along the road to Raikes Farm. From here more waymarks direct us over six stiles (we need to bear down left after the second) to the romantically named Snotterdale and then, one field later, we rejoin the road, turn right and continue back to our start.

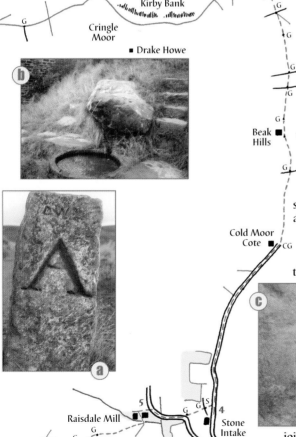

Special Interest – WALK 11

Bilsdale Valley stretches for about 10 miles from Newgate Bank north to Clay Bank. From Chop Gate, Raisdale forms a separate branch of the dale, though map-readers should be careful to note that Raisdale itself is further split and the O.S. map labels both the tributary valleys above Raisdale Mill as 'Raisdale'. Walkers completing Walk 11 have the chance to explore other parts of the dale after they have finished the walk itinerary. A visit to Spout House is especially worthwhile.

The valley bottom of Bilsdale is made up largely of shale rocks from the Lower Jurassic period and it was during this time that the ironstone, alum shales and layers of jet were laid down. These minerals were all later mined in Bilsdale. In later Middle Jurassic times successive layers of sand were deposited and these became the sandstone rocks seen on the steep valley sides. These rocks formed the building material for most of the houses in Bilsdale.

Though Bilsdale is tightly enclosed on its eastern and western sides, the glacial overflow gap in the Cleveland Hills at **Clay Bank** in the north has provided the dale with an important through route linking the Cleveland Plain and Teesside with Helmsley and the Vale of Pickering. During the construction of the Clay Bank car park, a prehistoric burial site was unearthed.

Signs of early settlement in Bilsdale may be seen in the **line of earthworks** skirting round the edge of Urra Moor. This must originally have been an impressive piece of engineering, though the date and function of the structure are debateable. Some writers have suggested it might be part of a Bronze Age defence system; others that it could have been the boundary of a medieval deer park or hunting area.

Place-name evidence shows that Bilsdale was certainly settled by the Scandinavians but it was the expansion of monastic activities in the 12th century that led to the vale's increased economic importance. In the south, **Rievaulx Abbey** acquired large areas of land and used the system of granges (or outlying farmsteads) to develop its sheep farming. Rievaulx also obtained most of the Raisdale area in the northwest of the dale. However, the land in the north-centre, including the settlements of Town Green and Seave Green, was given in 1200, not to Rievaulx, but to **Kirkham Priory**. Cold Moor Ridge, along part of which we travel on Walk 11, formed the boundary separating the Kirkham and Rievaulx lands.

Relations between the two monastic houses were not always cordial – a document from 1280 records how the Prior of Kirkham was accused by the Abbot of Rievaulx of 'cutting down and carrying off the Abbot's trees in his wood in Bilsdale'.

Ironstone exists in four poor quality seams in Bilsdale and the sites of a number of medieval bloomeries have been identified in the valley. In addition, iron smelting sites have been found at the two monastic granges of Grange and Laskill. The furnace at Laskill was of major significance, being stone-built, about four metres square in size and probably water-powered.

Jet was extensively mined in Bilsdale in the 19th century and the shale tips along the valley sides are a reminder of this activity, as they were along the valley sides of Scugdale on Walk 10. The stretch of land between Hasty Bank and Garfit was especially rich and here adits were not necessary.

St Hilda's Church, north of Chop Gate, is on a site that has been used for worship since about 1122. An inscribed stone, discovered in 1813 during repair work and now displayed above the porch doorway, tells of the involvement of William l'Espec in the original foundation of the church. A translation of the inscription reads: 'Lord William builds this church in honour of the chaste virgin St Hilda'. Major restoration work was needed in 1851 when the old building was taken down and replaced with a church built in the Victorian Gothic style.

Chop Gate Chapel was built to meet the growing needs of Methodists in Bilsdale in the 19th century. But it was not easy for Non-Conformists to obtain property in the valley until a private landowner sold them enough land (at five shillings a square yard) for the chapel to be built and then opened in 1858.

St John's Church at Fangdale Beck is little over a century old and was built by the then Earl of Feversham to serve the community in the southern end of Bilsdale.

Spout House is an especially good example of a 16th century cruck-framed cottage. Built in 1550 as a farm tenant's dwelling, it was licensed as an alehouse in 1714 and became the (old) Sun Inn. Two hundred years later, a larger building was needed and in 1914 the (new) Sun Inn was opened across the farmyard. The old Sun Inn/Spout House has been restored by the National Park. Traditional methods and materials have been used, although there has been no attempt to put back the 26 layers of wallpaper that were found in some places! A visit is highly recommended.

Stones: The Wain Stones are formed in the massive sandstone of the Ravenscar Group of rocks and with their broken, craggy cliff faces are an obvious attraction for climbers.

Special Interest – WALK 12

St Andrew's Church, Ingleby Greenhow has an interesting history. It is not certain whether there was a church on the site at the time of the Domesday Survey, even though the settlements of Ingleby and Greenhow are named in the Survey. The building we see today contains evidence of the Norman influence in, for example, the chancel arch and the nave arcade. There used to be an apse to the church but this was destroyed when the present chancel was built in the 1400s. Several centuries later, in 1741, much greater alterations were made and then in 1905 extensive repairs were again necessary. It was during these renovations that the remains of a Bos Torus (the extinct wild ox) were discovered under the floor.

Two stone effigies along the north aisle are of interest and the amusing carvings on the arcade columns remind us that church sculptors were sometimes allowed a fairly wide brief in their choice of subject matter. More details of the church's history and artefacts can be found in the guide leaflet.

Heather Moorland, the National Park information board reminds us, is a globally rare ecosystem and provides very good habitat for ground nesting birds such as curlew, lapwing, merlin and golden plover as well as grouse. Red grouse, as native birds, are unique to Britain and Ireland even though they are closely related to the willow grouse of Norway. They rely for food almost entirely on heather, eating different parts of the plant from winter until the seeds drop in autumn. In summer the long-legged St Mark's Fly appears in huge numbers on the moors. Britain is thought to have almost 75% of the world's remaining heather moorland and the North York Moors has the largest single continuous area in England. It is therefore a cause of grave concern when accidental moorland fires sweep across the terrain.

Incline Top used to be called 'Siberia' by the ironstone railway workers and it is easy to imagine this remote location being pretty breezy in mid-winter. Wagons full of iron ore went down the incline under gravity and this allowed empty wagons to be pulled back up at the same time.

The Face Stone has a crude carving of a face on its shaft and stands at the junction of several ancient roads. It is mentioned in 1642 as 'the bounder called Faceston' on the Streete Way. A similar stone in York Museum has been dated as late Bronze or early Iron Age.

Jenny Bradley's Cross is located where the ancient Thurkilsti track joins the Rudland Rigg road. Next to the broken cross stands a tall boundary stone marking the beginning of the Ingleby Estate. Who Jenny Bradley was is unclear, though 'Bradley' may be a corruption of 'breadlesse' which was the name for a beggar.

Special Interest – WALK 13

St Cuthbert's Church, Kildale There has been a church in Kildale since Anglo-Saxon times but Kildale is particularly interesting because here there is a record of pagan Viking burials at a Christian site. This is very unusual. During church excavations in 1868 a Viking sword, axe and weighing scales were uncovered in a burial site below the church floor. Remains of ancient standing crosses can be seen on the floor of the church tower and other old stones have been built into the outside of the porch. As an expression of the present vitality of the church and village, a delightful memorial stained glass window was installed in 1997. Outside the churchyard, we should notice the stone slabs of an ancient trod.

Kildale In Norman times, a motte and bailey castle was built just to the west of the church. The castle site is now occupied by a farm but the remains of the castle moat can still be seen and this is used in part by the present day railway line. Kildale Hall is a late Georgian mansion that was built where the old village used to be. The village at one time had a bleach mill on the River Leven and although floods swept this away, Bleach Mill Farm still exists. Kildale Estate has been in the hands of only three families since the time of the Norman Conquest.

John Wesley's Memorial Stone in the centre of Kildale village marks the site of a tree under which John Wesley is said to have preached in about 1772.

WALK 11
COLD MOOR –
URRA MOOR

Map: Explorer OL 26
S.E.P.T.: Chop Gate car park (559993)
Buses: 199, M2, M9
Cleveland Way distance: **3.1 miles**
Circular walk distance: **10.2 miles**
Shorter walk alternatives:
    North loop **7.1 miles**
    (from Clay Bank)
    South loop **7.1 miles**
Special interest: Bilsdale
Cross or Stone: Wain Stones (559035)

On this walk around the northern end of Bilsdale we make our way gradually up to the edge of the Cleveland Hills then follow a roller-coaster course up (and down) three steep summits on the CW before finishing with a fine walk along the edge of Urra Moor overlooking the Bilsdale valley. A shorter circuit northern loop, passing through the hamlet of Urra, can be walked from the car park at Clay Bank.

The long walk starts from Chop Gate car park where there are toilets and Moorsbus access. Leaving the car park we go left up the B1257 road into Chop Gate. At the war memorial we turn left towards Carlton in Cleveland and then immediately right on the p.r.o.w. past the Methodist chapel and up the sunken hollow-way called Cold Moor Lane. This can be muddy after heavy rain but is delightful in June.

The track opens out and after a little while we reach open moorland (1). Though the path soon divides, it joins up again and we have a gentle climb up through the heather and bilberry on to Cold Moor. After the track flattens out we pass the Three Howes tumuli and then reach the path crossing at (2) where the shorter northern loop walk joins in. Turning off left, just

before the grouse butts, we zigzag down the hillside towards Beak Hills Farm but immediately before the farm buildings we turn right on the green lane track along which we came (in the opposite direction) on Walk 10. This leads us to the CW fingerpost at (3) where we need to turn right.

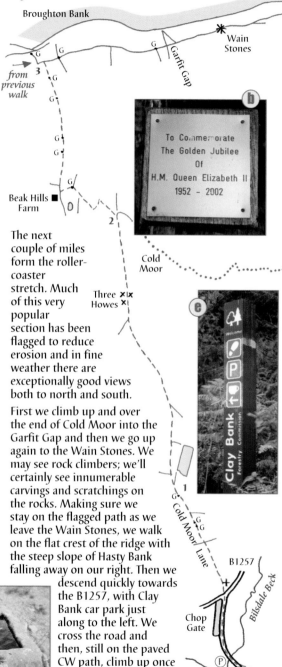

The next couple of miles form the roller-coaster stretch. Much of this very popular section has been flagged to reduce erosion and in fine weather there are exceptionally good views both to north and south.

First we climb up and over the end of Cold Moor into the Garfit Gap and then we go up again to the Wain Stones. We may see rock climbers; we'll certainly see innumerable carvings and scratchings on the rocks. Making sure we stay on the flagged path as we leave the Wain Stones, we walk on the flat crest of the ridge with the steep slope of Hasty Bank falling away on our right. Then we descend quickly towards the B1257, with Clay Bank car park just along to the left. We cross the road and then, still on the paved CW path, climb up once more.

When the path divides (and the flagstones end) just beyond the gate at (4) we have a problem. In order to complete the CW and to link up with the next walk we have to continue for about 1200m along Carr Ridge to the path crossing at (5) where we should turn right across the heather to (6). There is a p.r.o.w. over the heather but, unlike the path going left at (5), it is, at the time of writing, neither waymarked nor visible. Unless the heather has recently been cleared, it will be difficult to cross. So if we want to claim that we have completed all the CW, we either have to walk an out-and-back between (4) and (5) or try our luck tramping across the heather to (6). However, if we decide to miss out the CW section between (4) and (5), we branch right at the fingerpost at (4) and follow the bridleway to (6).

Continuing from (6), we go across a small valley and then carry on beside the ancient earthwork dividing the upland of Urra Moor from the steep valley slopes of Bilsdale until we come to the fingerpost and bridleway at (7). Here the short walk goes down the steep moorland edge to Urra while the longer route carries on for nearly two miles along the edge of the moorland. (In an emergency, or if weather conditions deteriorate, there are a number of escape routes from off the moorland edge and down to the valley floor.) Looking back, we have good views of the switchback we walked a short time ago.

When we come to the track crossing at (8) there is a choice of route. We can use the narrow p.r.o.w. going straight ahead and rising through the bracken until it joins the wide sandy game-shooters' track some 400m further ahead (9). Alternatively if the bracken is high we may wish to turn left up the slope and follow the clearer path up to the shooters' track. Whichever option we take, we bear right at the track and then keep going south to the junction by the stone wall at (10). A path leads off right but we stay on the main track swinging left for 70m before turning sharp right at grouse butt number 9.

About 230m further on we turn right again at the old waymark post then go through a gate in the dry stone wall. A clear path takes us down from the moorland over Black Intake to Wilham Beck Farm and from here a gated farm road leads towards the B1257. Just before the road, though, we cut off a corner by taking the path diagonally across the last field on our right. The Chop Gate car park is then a short distance to our right.

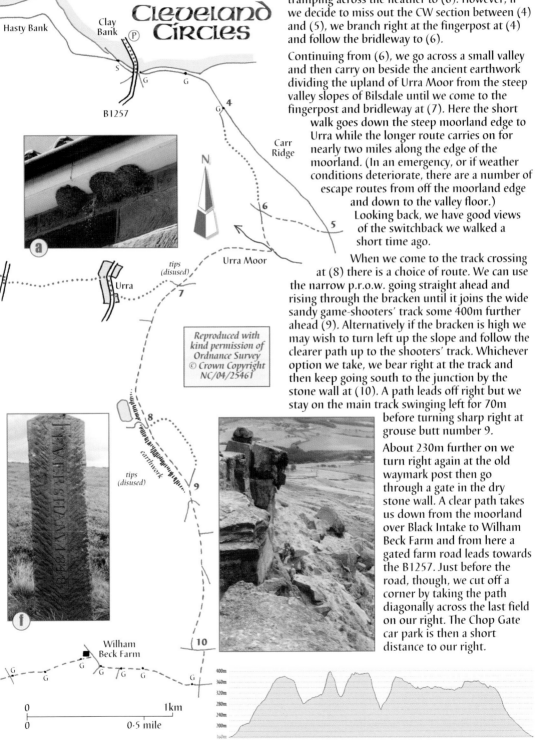

Reproduced with kind permission of Ordnance Survey © Crown Copyright NC/04/25461

WALK 12
URRA MOOR –
BATTERSBY MOOR

Map: Explorer OL 26
S.E.P.: Ingleby Greenhow Church (581062)
Bus: 84 Rail to Battersby Junction
Cleveland Way distance: **5.5 miles**
Circular walk distance: **10.5 miles**
Medium walk alternatives:
        North loop   **7.9 miles**
        South loop   **6.5 miles**
Shorter walk alternative:
        N.E. circuit   **5.9 miles**
Special interest:
    Moorland Marker Stones
Cross or Stone: Face Stone (597014)

This walk has everything a Cleveland Circle should have: terrific views, an ancient church, a stone circle (of sorts), moorland crosses, a short cut alternative and ... just one steep climb. For those walking the medium length northern and southern loops there is adequate roadside parking at the track leading to High Farm. Parking by the trackside south of Bank Foot Farm is possible for the short N.E. circuit. For this walk, the F.C. track (Alternative A on map) is more attractive than the p.r.o.w. (Alternative B on map).

The longer walk starts in Ingleby Greenhow at St Andrew's Church where there is parking, except on Sundays, for about five cars.

We go down the lane to the stepping stones (or through the churchyard to the footbridge) to cross Ingleby Beck and then take the steps on the other side going up on our left. Bending left (1) we continue along the field edge above the Ingleby Plantation and in springtime may be treated to a fine display of bluebells before the waymarked path leaves the side of the wood and crosses two fields to De L'Isle Cottage and then carries on over a couple more fields to Low Farm. Turning right to the minor road, we then go left along a quiet country lane, pass the starting point for the two medium length walks, and continue to New Sheepfold Farm.

From here the tarmac changes to a rough track, turning sharp right after some 400m. However, we leave this track where it swings left at (2) and instead go through the gate immediately ahead of us to follow the

grassy path, through another two gates, up to Greenhow Plantation. Now comes the only steep ascent on the walk as we take the waymarked p.r.o.w. going up the hill straight ahead of us. After crossing two broad forest rides (and taking a right-left turn at the second) we soon leave the trees and continue up and round over the moor to the Cleveland Way at (3).

We turn left and navigation is simple as we follow the CW for the next five and a half miles over wonderful heather grouse moor. But we should be alert and not miss the numerous intriguing marker stones along the way. The first one we pass is the Hand Stone (4) which is close to the trig point on Round Hill, the highest point on the North York Moors and so worthy of a short peak-bagging diversion. The summit is the site of a Bronze Age tumulus. A little further along the track is the enigmatic Face Stone (5) and then when we come to the Red Stone at Cockayne Head we may ponder on the reasons why people leave coins up here in the middle of nowhere. A little way beyond the Red Stone a short-cut track leads off left but we stay on the main CW, dropping just a little to cross High Bloworth stream before continuing on the flagged path up to dismantled Rosedale ironstone railway at (6).

A right turn on the disused track takes us to the old Bloworth Crossing (7). Here the Lyke Wake Walk and Coast to Coast trails carry straight on but we turn back left on ourselves and follow the CW along the ancient trackway coming from Rudland Rigg. The remains of Jenny Bradley's Cross and its replacement (8) cannot be missed. A short way further on when we spot a number of wooden posts over to our left, we can make a quick detour to see the highly recommended view from Incline Top. The shorter walk goes down the Incline but the longer circuit continues on the CW.

The hand stone dated 1757 at (9) and the marker stone for 'Greenh ... Road' at (10) remind us how important this ancient roadway has been through the centuries. At the gate and fingerpost where the track divides, the CW bears right and we follow this to the small cairn at the track crossing at (11). The track going off right is obvious. However we take the path on the left which is less clear at first but soon becomes wider. Going straight ahead past a cairn, we

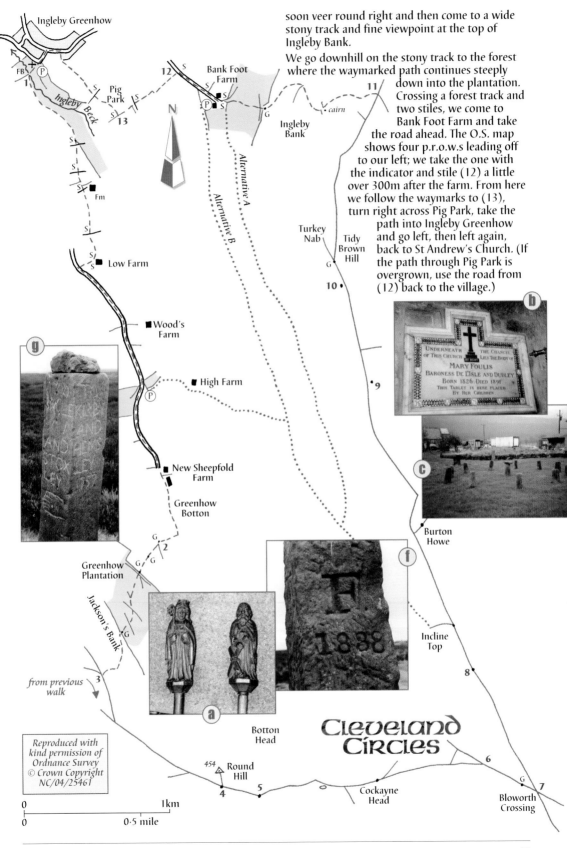

soon veer round right and then come to a wide stony track and fine viewpoint at the top of Ingleby Bank.

We go downhill on the stony track to the forest where the waymarked path continues steeply down into the plantation. Crossing a forest track and two stiles, we come to Bank Foot Farm and take the road ahead. The O.S. map shows four p.r.o.w.s leading off to our left; we take the one with the indicator and stile (12) a little over 300m after the farm. From here we follow the waymarks to (13), turn right across Pig Park, take the path into Ingleby Greenhow and go left, then left again, back to St Andrew's Church. (If the path through Pig Park is overgrown, use the road from (12) back to the village.)

Ingleby Greenhow

FB
P
Pig Park
13
Ingleby Beck
Fm
Low Farm
Wood's Farm
High Farm
P
New Sheepfold Farm
Greenhow Botton
Greenhow Plantation
Jackson's Bank
from previous walk
3
2

N

12
Bank Foot Farm
P
Ingleby Bank
cairn
11
Alternative A
Alternative B
Turkey Nab
Tidy Brown Hill
10
9
Burton Howe
Incline Top
8
6
Bloworth Crossing
7
Botton Head
Round Hill
454
4
5
Cockayne Head

CLeVeLanD CírcLes

Reproduced with kind permission of Ordnance Survey © Crown Copyright NC/04/25461

0   1km
0   0·5 mile

UNDERNEATH THE CHANCEL OF THIS CHURCH LIES THE BODY OF MARY FOULIS BARONESS DE L'ISLE AND DUDLEY BORN 1826 DIED 1891 THIS TABLET IS HERE PLACED BY HER CHILDREN

F 1888

WALK 13
BATTERSBY MOOR –
CAPTAIN COOK'S
MONUMENT

Map: Explorer OL 26
S.E.P.:   Kildale (607093). Toilets in Kildale
        cafés
Buses: 27, 84 Rail to Kildale
Cleveland Way distance: **5.0 miles**
Circular walk distance: **11.5 miles**
Medium walk alternatives:
      North loop   **8.4 miles**
      South loop   **5.2 miles**
Short north loop: **5.2 miles**
Special interest:
    Kildale village, Cook Monument
Cross or Stone:
    John Wesley Memorial (608094)

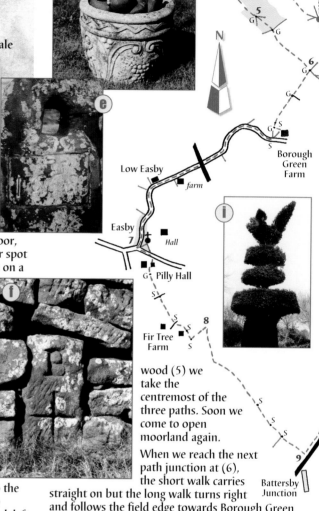

With its commanding position on Easby Moor,
Captain Cook's Monument is a very popular spot
for day outings and has already been visible on a
number of earlier CC walks. Both the long
and the short options for Walk 13 begin
at Kildale but those preferring to do two
medium distance loops could commence
both from Battersby.

Assuming we start from Kildale, where
there is parking for half a dozen cars, it's
probably a good idea to visit St Cuthbert's
Church, by the railway station, on an out-
and-back diversion before doing the rest
of the walk.

Returning from the church, the CW
fingerpost directs us left at Glebe Cottage
Tea Rooms. The road goes under the
railway and then continues up to and
past Bankside Farm up the steep gradient to the
top of the road at (1). Here we turn left into
Coate Moor Woods and, remembering to fork left
off the main track at the indicator (2), follow the
wide, level F.C. track for a little over a mile to
Captain Cook's Monument.

Half a dozen paths converge at the summit and
we leave by the one going N.W. – that's the first
one to the left of the paved CW track – and we
aim for the two free-standing gateposts visible at
the first field boundary. We soon turn left at a
waymark (3) and then the path plunges steeply
down through the trees ahead. We come to a
forest ride where we go right for about 100m and
then turn left to leave the wood. Following the
wall, we join the bridleway at (4) and here go left
again.

After 50m or so, we bear left where the path splits
and when we reach the gate at the edge of the

wood (5) we
take the
centremost of the
three paths. Soon we
come to open
moorland again.

When we reach the next
path junction at (6),
the short walk carries
straight on but the long walk turns right
and follows the field edge towards Borough Green
Farm. Just before the farm, waymarks direct us
via gate and stile to a narrow road. We turn right
and walk for almost a mile through Low Easby
and then on to the junction in Easby (7).

We turn left on the road and then quickly go right
on the drive (not signposted in 2005) into Pilly
Hall Farm. A waymarked gate at the end of the
farmyard gives our direction to a second gate and
then across a field to a stile. From here we go over
another field (aim for the telegraph pole) and
need to keep close to the hedge round the large
house on our right in order not to miss the next
two stiles. Next we skirt round to the left of Fir
Tree Farm, cross a double stile, turn sharp left to
the field corner (8) and here, turning right and
keeping to the edge of the field, walk towards
Battersby Junction.

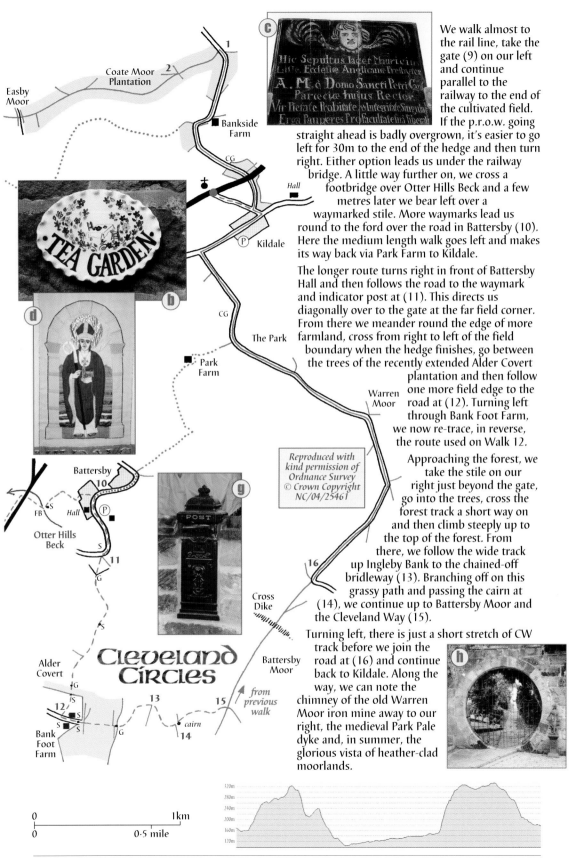

We walk almost to the rail line, take the gate (9) on our left and continue parallel to the railway to the end of the cultivated field. If the p.r.o.w. going straight ahead is badly overgrown, it's easier to go left for 30m to the end of the hedge and then turn right. Either option leads us under the railway bridge. A little way further on, we cross a footbridge over Otter Hills Beck and a few metres later we bear left over a waymarked stile. More waymarks lead us round to the ford over the road in Battersby (10). Here the medium length walk goes left and makes its way back via Park Farm to Kildale.

The longer route turns right in front of Battersby Hall and then follows the road to the waymark and indicator post at (11). This directs us diagonally over to the gate at the far field corner. From there we meander round the edge of more farmland, cross from right to left of the field boundary when the hedge finishes, go between the trees of the recently extended Alder Covert plantation and then follow one more field edge to the road at (12). Turning left through Bank Foot Farm, we now re-trace, in reverse, the route used on Walk 12.

Approaching the forest, we take the stile on our right just beyond the gate, go into the trees, cross the forest track a short way on and then climb steeply up to the top of the forest. From there, we follow the wide track up Ingleby Bank to the chained-off bridleway (13). Branching off on this grassy path and passing the cairn at (14), we continue up to Battersby Moor and the Cleveland Way (15).

Turning left, there is just a short stretch of CW track before we join the road at (16) and continue back to Kildale. Along the way, we can note the chimney of the old Warren Moor iron mine away to our right, the medieval Park Pale dyke and, in summer, the glorious vista of heather-clad moorlands.

Reproduced with kind permission of Ordnance Survey
© Crown Copyright NC/04/25461

Cleveland Circles

WALK 14
CAPTAIN COOK'S MONUMENT – HIGHCLIFF NAB

Map: Explorer OL 26
S.E.P.: Gribdale Gate car park (592110)
Buses to Great Ayton: 29, 81, 781, M2
         Rail to Great Ayton
Cleveland Way distance: **4.6 miles**
Circular walk distance: **10.4 miles**
Shorter walk alternatives:
         North loop   **4.8 miles**
         South loop   **5.6 miles**
Special interest:
    Roseberry Topping, Bold Venture Gill
    RIGS, Cliff Rigg Quarry, Captain Cook Trail
Cross or Stone: Cook's Monument (590101)

This is a fairly strenuous figure-of-eight walk with four short steep climbs but it can easily be split into two separate sections. The full figure-of-eight starts from Gribdale Gate car park while Hutton Village forms a suitable start for the northern loop. Train travellers start from Great Ayton Station.

Starting from Gribdale Gate we go north and climb the steps up the CW. We are soon on the edge of Great Ayton Moor and pass an important Neolithic Age chambered long cairn as we continue on the level surface round to the gate at the path junction (1).

Here the southern loop branches left through the gate towards Roseberry Topping while the longer walk stays on the CW, leaving the wall and cutting back at about 45° across the moor.

At the next gate (2) we come to the edge of Hanging Stone Wood, bear right and follow the edge of the forest for some 500m or so before striking right on to the moor again. After about 170m a waymarker post directs us left over to Black Nab and we make our way down on the partly flagged path towards Highcliffe Farm. The trail passes south of the farm before swinging up left into Guisborough Forest. We soon need to bear up right

and then the CW meets the Tees Link track. Now we turn left on this wide track down to the path intersection at (3). Again turning left, we stay on the Tees Link, go through the F.C. gate and then enter woodland once more. The way winds through the trees and then we pass an information board giving details of the Bold Venture Gill R.I.G.S.

Very soon after this the Tees Link goes down sharp right (4) and this is where the

Cleveland Circles

Reproduced with kind permission of Ordnance Survey © Crown Copyright NC/04/25461

0 ———————————— 1km
0 ———————————— 0·5 mile

from previous walk

shorter walk (north loop) comes up from Hutton Village. However, the longer walk stays left but then quickly swings right and our route on the broad forest trail stays level for the next 1.5 miles making two broad sweeps southwards to avoid two deep stream valleys.

We need to be watchful to see the waymark on the right at (5) and then, after 25m, we leave the main track and take the path on our left up the steep slope to the Hanging Stone. Using the excuse to survey the panorama of Guisborough and beyond, we stop for a breather a few metres further on. Then we continue, walking between lines of trees, before bearing right at the U-fork (6). But almost immediately we need to keep left to avoid the path going down steeply on our right. When we come to the edge of the forest, we cross the stile, carry on parallel to the wall and arrive back at the path intersection (1).

To complete the figure-of-eight, we go through the gate, bend down left and then climb the steep ascent of Roseberry Topping. Views from the top can be terrific but the drop is perilous.

A considerable number of paths radiate from the summit and we need to be careful in choosing our descent. We aim for the summer house with its minaret-like roof to the south-west. To get there, we need to retrace steps for 20m to the two iron posts

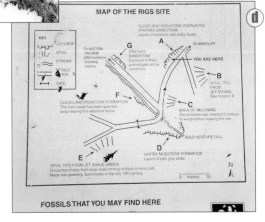

and then take the paved path forking right (i.e., not the one we came up on) which quickly curves round towards the summer house. With the minaret on our left, we go down a wide gulley with gorse bushes on either side to the gate into Newton Wood (7).

Following the fence and crossing a small stream, and then avoiding a fork up left, we are led gently down, past

MAP OF THE RIGS SITE

FOSSILS THAT YOU MAY FIND HERE

several paths going back on our left, to the turning at (8), just a short distance away from the railway line. We turn back sharp left on the broad track but after 100m must be careful to branch off left up into the trees. This path through Cliff Ridge Wood has a gorgeous display of springtime bluebells and up to our left we can see remains of the former whinstone quarrying.

At the end of the wood we follow the edge of a field to Aireyholme Lane (9). Here we turn right and walk down the road to the junction with Dikes Lane.

Crossing straight over we continue on the bridleway to the field corner at (10), turn left along the wall and come into Ayton Banks Wood. It's a fierce climb so near the end of a walk as we bear right up through the trees but, as we've said before, 'the views are worth it'. Just after the end of the wood the path turns right for a few hundred metres to Captain Cook's Monument and from there we turn north (left) on the paved CW again back down to our start.

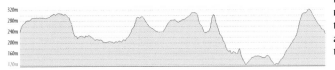

Special Interest – WALK 14

Roseberry Topping in snow

Roseberry Topping is an outlier separated by a deep col from Newton Moor. The sandstone capping of the hill has slipped as a result of mining for ironstone in the underlying Lias shale rocks.

Bold Venture Gill is an **RIGS (Regionally Important Geological Site)** and has a rare inland exposure of Cleveland ironstone, Staithes sandstone and Whitby mudstone in which jet is found. At the information board we see the exposure of ironstone and the jet mining spoil tips.

The **Cleveland Dyke** (or Whinstone Ridge) is a line of igneous rock stretching across the Moors and continuing to the Isle of Mull in Scotland. It outcrops at **Cliff Rigg Quarry** and at several other locations. Quarrying for the resistant whinstone was mainly to provide road-building material but the Cliff Rigg Quarry finished extraction in 1973. It now provides a variety of different wildlife habitats.

The Captain Cook Trail is a 70-mile circular road tour linking four of the main places connected with the life of James Cook. The first of these locations is **Marton**, on the outskirts of Middlesbrough, where James was born in 1728 but Marton is a few miles distant from the Cleveland Way. However, the other three centres of Great Ayton, Staithes and Whitby are all either on or very close to Cleveland Circles itineraries.

The Cook family left Marton in 1736 and moved to Aireyholme Farm on the outskirts of **Great Ayton** where James grew up and received his education. Some years after James left home, the family moved into the village and James' father built his own cottage in Bridge Street. In the village, the Cook Schoolroom Museum recreates aspects of 18th century school life and in the graveyard of All Saints Church is the burial place of his mother and five of his siblings. The Church dates from 1123 when Robert de Meynell of Whorlton Castle granted land to Whitby Abbey. The Bridge Street cottage is no longer visible but the site is marked by a granite obelisk, brought from near the spot where Cook landed on his

voyage to Australia. Amazingly, the original cottage was dismantled, stone by stone, and transported to Melbourne in Australia where it was re-erected in 1934. Great Ayton is accessible from Walk 14.

Roger Eckersley, who, just by chance on holiday, was photographed outside the Melbourne cottage

James left home at 17 to work in a grocer's shop in **Staithes**. The shop is no longer there; not because it's gone to Australia, but because it was washed into the sea during a particularly fierce North Sea storm. Parts of the shop were re-built into what is today called 'Cook's Cottage' and we pass this on Walk 19. Such can be the ferocity of North Sea gales that a ship's bowsprit is reported to have once crashed through the window of the local pub. In the village we can find further details about Cook's achievements at the Captain Cook and Staithes Heritage Centre.

Cook soon moved to **Whitby** where he became apprenticed to the shipowner John Walker whose collier vessels carried coal to London. When we come to Whitby (Walks 21 and 22) we can discover more of Cook's exploits at the Memorial Museum in Grape Lane where James lived and also at the Whitby Museum in Pannett Park ... there's certainly no lack of effort spared in promoting Cleveland's favourite son!

Captain Cook is best remembered for his voyages of exploration to New Zealand and eastern Australia (1769-70) and then to the South Seas (1772). It was on his next voyage, searching for the North-west passage round northern Canada, that he was forced to rest in Owhyhee (Hawaii) where he was killed trying to settle a dispute between his men and the local people.

Stone: Captain Cook's Monument was erected on Easby Moor in 1827. It is a 15m high obelisk overlooking Marton, the suburb of Middlesbrough where James Cook was born, and Great Ayton where he went to school. 'A man' the inscription tells us, 'in nautical knowledge inferior to none.' The monument was struck by lightning in 1960.

Gisborough Priory – WALK 15

Gisborough Priory Although little else remains today, the magnificent arch at the east end of the former Priory Church is a reminder that this was once a superb Gothic structure and a wealthy medieval religious house. It was founded and richly endowed as a priory for Augustinian canons in about 1119 by Robert de Brus.

Around 1200 the Priory Church was rebuilt on a bigger scale so that the west end had twin towers, the aisles were floored with coloured tiles and the north aisle was divided into a series of small alcoves or private chapels. However, in 1289 the church was gutted by fire and the Priory lost all its books, plate and vestments. Scorch marks from the blaze have been identified on the paving between some of the pillars at the west end. Rebuilding the church took about 100 years but the Priory did eventually recover so that by the time of the Dissolution of the Monasteries by Henry VIII it had become, after the abbeys of York, Fountains and Selby, the fourth richest monastic house in Yorkshire. Prior Pursglove reportedly kept 'a most pompous house' before having to surrender the Priory to the King's men on Christmas Eve 1539. The site was later sold to Sir Thomas Chaloner in 1550 and he incorporated the remaining stonework into ornamental gardens for his own use. Today Gisborough Priory is in the hands of English Heritage.

Dan Savage

A

B

C

D

E

F

G

H

I

Each walk
has its own
Cross or Stone.
The key for
identification
is on page 107

LYKE
WAKE
WALK

L

J

K

O

M

N

and stones

P
Q
R
S
U
T
V
W
X
A.D. 2000
Y
AA
BB
Z
CC
THIS STONE MARKS THE SITE
OF A TREE UNDER WHICH
JOHN WESLEY
IS SAID TO HAVE PREACHED
c.1772
DD

1914

53

WALK 15
HIGHCLIFF NAB –
SLAPEWATH
(via GUISBOROUGH)

Map: Explorer OL 26
S.E.P.T.: Rectory Lane car park (615158)
Buses: X56, 781, M2, M11, M16
Cleveland Way distance: **3.5 miles**
Circular walk distance: **10.3 miles**
Shorter walk alternatives:
      West loop   **5.9 miles**
      East loop   **5.5 miles**
Special interest:
   Guisborough, Gisborough Priory,
   Cleveland Street
Cross: Guisborough Market Cross (615160)

The highlights of this walk are the superb views northwards from the CW and the evocative remains of Gisborough Priory. Two shorter circuits can be created by using the link from Butt Lane up through Guisborough Woods to the CW track. If this is done, parking for the western loop has to be in Hutton Village.

Assuming we are doing the longer walk, we start from the car park and toilets in Rectory Lane, Guisborough, walk east along Whitby Lane and turn right down Butt Lane (1). Tarred at first, this wide bridleway soon splits and we take the dirt track forking left. We swing left parallel to a disused railway, turn right over the rail track and are led up to the edge of the F.C. plantation at (2). Here the shorter walk goes straight ahead up into the woods. (A lot of contours! Make sure to go right up to the CW where five stone steps indicate the correct location.)

The long walk turns right and follows the path along the edge of the wood. We stay on this to the six-route junction at (3) and here we keep to the main wide track which, after 100m, bears slightly left and soon goes upwards into the trees. We ignore side paths leading off but at the triangular patch of greenery (4) we turn down steeply to the right and then swing round left at the bottom of the woods.

The forest track is broad and firm (and generally level) so progress is easy as we continue with a few twists and turns, but again ignoring all side-tracks, round to the road in Hutton Village (5). We have now joined the Tees Link and turning left, we go to the lamp-post at the Y-fork near the end of the houses and bear right.

Entering Guisborough Forest, the steep ascent is along the line of the old ironstone tramway. At the top of the slope we bend left and retrace the route, past the R.I.G.S. information board, which we took on Walk 14. We cross the open area where the F.C. at one time sold Christmas trees and then once more enter the woods. Again we ignore the paths leading off to either side but keep on the main track to the edge of the trees at (6).

We stay on this stony track as it turns up sharp right immediately after the F.C. half-gate. Then at the crossing (7) by the Tees Link indicator post we join the CW and, turning back sharp left, go up the slope to Highcliff Nab. There is a steep climb up the stone steps but the views from the top are a good excuse to stop for a break. Redcar's steelworks still steam away; Hartlepool's nuclear power station glistens in the sunlight; Saltburn snoozes peacefully.

For the next couple of miles we follow a wide, level track through woodland and even in a wet February, I found the surface surprisingly firm. About 1.5 miles from Highcliff Nab, we reach the bridleway crossing (8) where the link path between the two shorter walks descends to the north edge of the woods. At the time of writing there is a waymark showing the p.r.o.w. going up

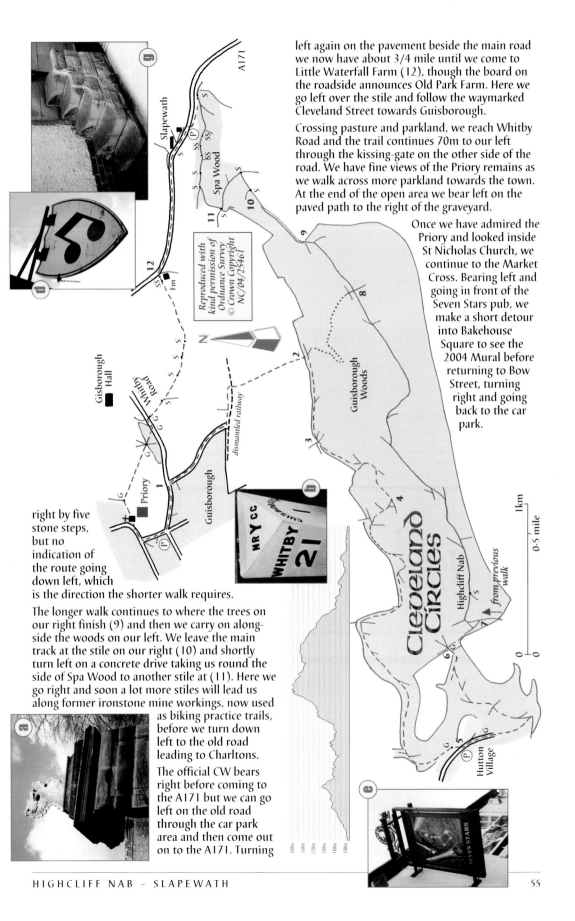

left again on the pavement beside the main road we now have about 3/4 mile until we come to Little Waterfall Farm (12), though the board on the roadside announces Old Park Farm. Here we go left over the stile and follow the waymarked Cleveland Street towards Guisborough.

Crossing pasture and parkland, we reach Whitby Road and the trail continues 70m to our left through the kissing-gate on the other side of the road. We have fine views of the Priory remains as we walk across more parkland towards the town. At the end of the open area we bear left on the paved path to the right of the graveyard.

Once we have admired the Priory and looked inside St Nicholas Church, we continue to the Market Cross. Bearing left and going in front of the Seven Stars pub, we make a short detour into Bakehouse Square to see the 2004 Mural before returning to Bow Street, turning right and going back to the car park.

right by five stone steps, but no indication of the route going down left, which is the direction the shorter walk requires.

The longer walk continues to where the trees on our right finish (9) and then we carry on along-side the woods on our left. We leave the main track at the stile on our right (10) and shortly turn left on a concrete drive taking us round the side of Spa Wood to another stile at (11). Here we go right and soon a lot more stiles will lead us along former ironstone mine workings, now used as biking practice trails, before we turn down left to the old road leading to Charltons.

The official CW bears right before coming to the A171 but we can go left on the old road through the car park area and then come out on to the A171. Turning

Special Interest – WALK 15

Guisborough, 'the ancient capital of Cleveland', has been a market town for over 700 years and today the market still operates three times a week. The Fox Inn can be traced back to the early 18th century when it was a coaching inn. The mounting steps, used for climbing up on to horse-drawn carriages, still stand outside the inn which was demolished and rebuilt in 1926.

In 1779, John Oxlee was born near Guisborough. A self-taught grammarian, he compiled an astonishing book in which our commonest English words are translated into 100 different languages.

Bakehouse Square, the site of the common bakehouse in medieval times, contains an imaginative mural and associated information board outlining aspects of the town's development.

St Nicholas Church, Guisborough
The Domesday Book of 1086 records a church in Guisborough but there is no structural evidence of this building today. The present chancel walls and tower are thought to have been built around 1500 but the nave and the interior have been much altered. Most of the present church results from the reconstruction of 1903-8 that was planned by Temple Moore and paid for by the parishioners.

St Nicholas was Bishop of Myra in the 4th century although little of certainty is known about him. His feast day is 6th December and has long been associated with the exchanging of gifts so that in the West he is associated, as 'Santa Claus', with the giving of presents on Christmas Day.

Inside the church, look for the figure of Christ in medieval glass, the mosaic floor tiles re-assembled from the Priory grounds and the De Brus cenotaph memorial constructed about 1520 to commemorate Robert de Brus, the founder of the Priory.

Cleveland Street is an old route between Guisborough and Loftus and sections of the waymarked trail will be used on Walks 16, 17, 18 as well as on the present circuit. Known at different times as 'Via de Witbei' and 'Back Street' it was once an important pedestrian highway, probably linking Gisborough Priory and Whitby Abbey. The section between Slapewath and Skinningrove gives fascinating reminders of East Cleveland's industrial heritage.

Guisborough Market Cross has a tapering shaft supporting a square block on each side of which is a design incorporating the numbers 1-12. The sphere above has the same numbers around it. The present cross was renovated in 1990.

Special Interest – WALK 16

The Margrove Valley has been the scene of various mining activities since **alum** was first obtained from the Rockhole Quarry at Slapewath in 1603/1604. However, inland sites such as Slapewath were at a disadvantage for sea transport compared with coastal locations like Boulby and Ravenscar. Nevertheless, when the alum working at Rockhole finished, the quarry was able to switch activity to **jet** mining.
Ironstone is rock containing iron ore and 'ironstone' is known to have been collected from North Sea beaches as early as 1748 but it was not until 100 years later with the discovery of ironstone at Loftus in 1848 that the actual mining of iron ore in Cleveland began. Easily the most

Decorative Gravel & Slate Bulk or Bags

important of the ironstone deposits was the Main Seam and this could be more than three metres thick. At first the ore was sent to blast furnaces on Teesside or Tyneside. The 'bord and pillar' system was the common way of working – 'bords' (passages) were first cut in the rock and then the miners worked back through the mine removing the 'pillars' that had been left standing. Many of the men were experienced miners from Wales and Cornwall but conditions were hard; they had to buy their own blasting powder and were only paid for actual time at the workface even if they had several miles to walk underground.

The Margrove Valley was an important location. Mining started here in 1863 at Aysdale Gate and other mines at Spa (1864) and Spa Wood (1865) were quickly opened. For a short time there were seven mines operating in the valley but economic difficulties in the 1920s and 1930s caused closures and Margrove's last mine (South Skelton) eventually shut in 1954, just ten years before mining stopped altogether in Cleveland.

Errington Wood, the car park information board tells us, was first settled over 6,000 years ago by Mesolithic hunter-gatherers with their microlithic arrowheads and scrapers. Evidence of later Bronze Age occupation includes the burial mound at the S.W corner of the woods.

In 1773 the Errington family created a commercial conifer plantation and then in 1850 ironstone was discovered in the woodland. Three separate drifts were dug into the hillside and Upleatham became the most productive of Cleveland's ironstone mines after Eston. New Marske was developed as a settlement to house the miners close to their work. The mining caused much subsidence and Upleatham lost its hall, though the church, under which working was prohibited, was spared. Since the mine closed in 1923 the area has been landscaped and planted with conifers but current management policy is to produce a mixed woodland which provides a greater variety of habitats for wildlife. Over 90 bird species have been recorded, including crossbill, siskin and goldcrest which are all associated with coniferous woodland.

Sandstone quarries within the wood were formerly used to supply local building stone.

Skelton Castle is today a large private house but a real castle stood on the site in Norman times. Robert de Brus had a castle here (with a moat some 70m wide), though it is possible the castle had been built before he acquired the land in about 1100. Legend suggests that the country's powerful barons met here to agree their strategy before forcing King John to sign the Magna Carta in 1215. Certainly Skelton was important in the 13th century; it was recorded as a borough in 1240; and the footpath leading north from the A173 to All Saints Church and the castle site is the former main street and is still known as Boroughgate Lane.

After the remains of the medieval castle had been pulled down and the site levelled, a new stately home was built on the site. The castellations date from about 1794, the period when mock fortifications were becoming a popular feature of large houses.

All Saints (Old) Church, Skelton has a churchyard where pirates' graves are found among the cherry trees and garlic. It is thought that two previous churches existed on the site but the present building was constructed in 1785 and includes some medieval masonry. It has been suggested that the herringbone tooling of the outside stonework gives a local flavour in contrast to the 'Venetian' east window. Pevsner records that inside are a three-decker pulpit, box pews, a barrel organ and a family pew - with a fireplace. An ancient Anglo-Saxon sundial found in the cemetery is housed in All Saints (New) Church, built in 1884.

Upleatham Church is also disused. It has been said to be the smallest church (18 x 15 feet) in the country, though the claim is a little misleading since the building was originally much bigger than it is today. It was partly demolished in 1822 and replaced by a new church higher up the hill, but the 1684 tower was kept and used as a mortuary chapel. In 1966 soldiers of the Green Howards cleaned, repaired and restored the building.

Tockett's Mill is a fine example of a restored, working, water-driven corn mill that is open to the public on Sunday afternoons in summer. It claims to be one of the most complete mills in the country, with its four floors containing the original machinery as well as an extensive collection of equipment from other mills.

The remains of what may be **Skelton Market Cross** stand as an upright post in a raised flower-bed on the old village green. On two of the sides of the pillar are thin strips of metal. Some say it is the shaft of a true market cross, though others maintain it is remnant of the old whipping post, the victim having been tied to the metal strips.

WALK 16
SLAPEWATH – SKELTON

Map: Explorer OL 26
S.E.P.: Car park adjacent to A171 near
           Slapewath (643157)
Buses: 28, 93, 93A, M2
Cleveland Way distance: **2.6 miles**
Circular walk distance: **12.5 miles**
           (incl Upleatham loop)
           9.5 miles
           (excl Upleatham loop)
Shorter walk alternative: **4.7 miles**
           (using Cleveland Street)
Special interest:
     Tockett's Mill, Margrove Valley, Errington
     Wood, Skelton Church and Castle
Cross: Skelton Market Cross (655188)

From the former mining area of Slapewath we
follow the CW to Skelton. The circular walk then
goes across farm country to Upleatham and
Errington Wood returning via the restored
Tocketts Mill and the aptly named Mucky Lane. A
shorter alternative is possible if the 'Upleatham
Loop' is omitted while a much shorter route can
be walked if we return from Skelton to Slapewath
along Cleveland Street.

We leave from the western end of the Slapewath
car park (by the bus stop), turn left, cross the
A171 and walk to the second turning leading to
the terrace of houses that forms Slapewath. CW
markers direct us forward over two stiles and then
we bend right to follow the path through gorse-
bracken scrub round the edge and up to the top of
Rockhole Quarry (1).

The CW turns right along the top of Rawcliff Bank
and then at the stile (2) we go right again. The
track is obvious and after Airy Hill Farm it runs
generally downhill! At Skelton Green the longer
walks cross straight over Boosbeck Road (3) whilst
the shorter circuit turns right on the road before
turning right again on to Cleveland Street.

Longer walkers continue on the tarred path,
spotting Skelton Castle down left, round to
The Hills and then down the steps into
Skelton High Street (4). Now we turn left and
at the traffic lights (5) follow the A173
towards Guisborough.

We should not miss the opportunity to visit
All Saints Old Church on our right. Then we
continue with care on the grass verge beside
the busy A173 to the step-stile immediately
after the drive to Barns Farm and cross a field
to a second stile. Following the field edge we come
to a gap at the corner (6) above the wooded valley
of Skelton Beck. The path down left and then along
the beck-side is clear, though perhaps muddy, and
after crossing the second footbridge we go left for
50m to a stile and here leave the stream to head
up towards the tower of Upleatham Church.

From the churchyard we turn left on the B1268
road, pass Capon Hall Farm and take the side road
on our right (7) up to Upleatham village. Turning
left, we walk to the end of the buildings and
follow the wide p.r.o.w. going on ahead into the
trees. On our left is a Wellingtonia, the world's
largest tree species.

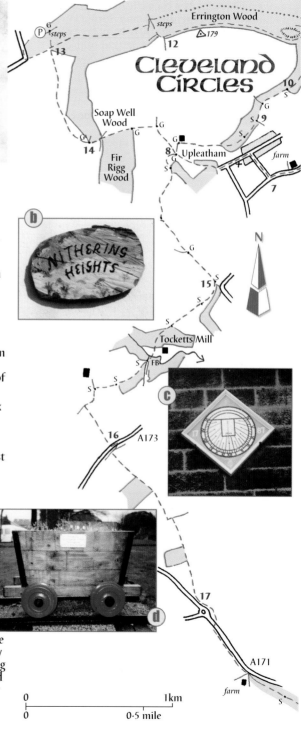

Cleveland Circles

0 ——————————————— 1km
0 ————————————— 0·5 mile

Just after the gate we come to a path junction (8). Here the medium distance walk turns left but those choosing to include the Upleatham loop go right and very shortly need to go right again through the gate just before the farm buildings. The path goes along field edges and then into Village Wood. We bear left at the stile-and-steps junction (9) then right a little further on, go through the gate and alongside a couple more fields before entering the trees again (10).

We stay on the p.r.o.w. as far as the path intersection at (11) and here we have a choice of routes. There are many tracks in Errington Wood and although not all are p.r.o.w.s, the public is permitted to use them. I prefer to turn immediately left, climbing up and then following the edge of the wood, passing the trig point over to our left and going as far as the field corner at (12).

We turn right and go down to the bottom of the steps. Turning left, then quickly swinging right, we take the bridle track back to the crossing at (13). A right turn would take us to the car park, so instead we turn left and continue on Sandy Lane to the gate at (14). After the gate the path soon splits – we bear right keeping Fir Rigg Wood on our right. Soon we go through another gate and then at the path T-junction turn right. When we reach the intersection at (8), where we were earlier on the walk, we branch right to follow the wide farm track over pastureland dotted with trees. At the stile about 40m before the road bend (15) we go right again on a narrow path and must not miss the third stile leading left down through the trees to Tocketts Beck.

We can make a slight diversion to see the restored mill to our left before we cross the tarmac bridge over the river and then soon take the path over the footbridge on our right. The route follows the edge of the wood and goes along one field as far as the track to Tocketts House. Here we turn left, swing quickly right and then turn sharp left again to reach the A173 at (16).

The path on the other side of the road is slightly offset to our left and then, after crossing the old road, we travel along Mucky Lane for about a mile to the roundabout (17) on the A171. Bending left, we use the pavement on the right-hand side of the road to bring us to the bus stop by Little Waterfall Farm.

From here we take the footpath branching off right which leads us under the bridge of the old Cleveland Railway, past the Waterfall Viaduct and up to Spawood Ironstone Mine. We walk behind the old office buildings (now a house) and then notice the blocked off drift entrance to the mine and the powder house, located away from the rest of the site for safety reasons. Soon we re-join the CW and carry on past the broad terrace below which was Spa Mine and then we arrive back at our starting point.

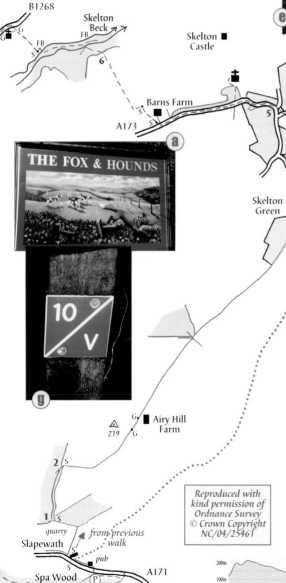

WALK 17
SKELTON –
SKINNINGROVE

Cleveland Way distance:	**6.0 miles**
Circular walk distance:	**10.8 miles**
Shorter walk alternatives:	
West loop	**6.8 miles**
Central loop	**6.0 miles**
East loop	**5.0 miles**

Map: Explorer OL 26
S.E.P.T.: Saltburn car park (668216) or roadside in Skelton
Bus: X4, 62, 48, 49, M16
Rail to Saltburn

Special interest:
Saltburn Valley & Rift's Wood, Tom Leonard Museum, Nature Reserves
Cross or Stone:
Cleveland Coast carved stone (671215)

This walk follows the very attractive valley of Skelton Beck into Saltburn and then continues along the North Sea cliff top to Skinningrove. The Cleveland Street brings us back to Skelton. The shorter west loop uses the valley of Saltburn Gill while the shorter east loop crosses Hunley Hall Golf Club.

We will assume a start from Skelton, continuing the itinerary description from High Street (1) where we left the CW on Walk 16. Going down Coniston Road, a CW diversion at the library takes

the first road right (Derwent Road) and this leads us through the built-up area to the edge of the houses at (2). We bear left through the

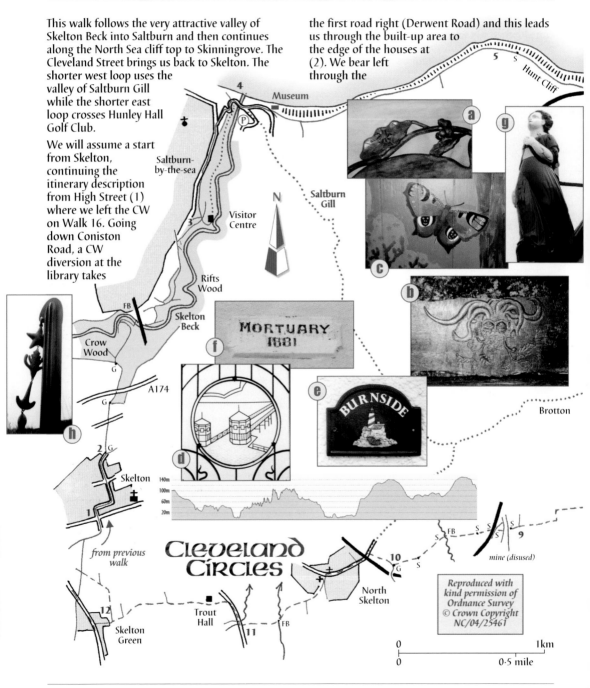

MORTUARY 1881

BURNSIDE

Cleveland Circles

0   1km
0   0·5 mile

kissing-gate to cross two fields; though new house building may alter this; and the path then goes through recent development and is waymarked to go under the A174 Skelton bypass.

On entering Crow Wood, the scenery becomes much more agreeable and the CW leads down steps to Skelton Beck. We double back on ourselves and are led over an iron footbridge and then, bearing right under the massive arches of the railway viaduct, we take a delightful path through Rifts Wood.

The first path off right leads down to the remains of Marske Mill but we stay on the main track and ignore side-paths until we come to the tarmac at (3). In order to stay on the CW we must go left and up the slope to Saltburn's Albion Terrace, then bear right and then right again down Glenside towards the sea. However, if preferred, we can go down right at the path junction to the Visitor Centre and then make our way on one of several paths through the Valley Gardens and beside

road and, hopefully, we will have time to visit the Smugglers' Heritage Centre next to The Ship before leaving the road and taking the left hand path up the steep slope towards Hunt Cliff. At the top, we have three miles or so of gently undulating, exhilarating cliff top walking.

We pass Hunt Cliff Nature Reserve (5) and then contour round the side of Warsett Hill (there are two hills with this name on the O.S. map). Here we walk immediately next to the rail line carrying Boulby potash to Teesside and soon pass the remains of the old Huntcliff fan house which helped ventilate the ironstone mine workings below. Those completing the shorter eastern circuit can now use the stile at (6) to cross the N.T. open access land before continuing on the p.r.o.w. over Hunley Hall Golf Club.

After 0.8 mile, we descend the steps to Cattersty Sands and continue along the beach towards Skinningrove. Just before we come into the settlement, we turn right up some concrete steps and then continue left along Marine Terrace to the bridge over Kilton Beck (7).

Turning right at the bridge, we follow the road through the village, going right-left through The Square and then take the path left of the play area to the Tom Leonard Mining Museum (8).

Leaving the museum car park at the far exit, we go across Kilton Beck again and just ahead is a marker post directing us right along the Cleveland Street Walk. We'll follow this waymarked route for the next three miles. Rising steeply out of the Kilton valley we cross the line of one of the region's numerous dismantled railways before reaching a minor road where we bear left and then soon go directly over the A174 road. The route goes along Front Street, into Steavenson Street and on, past the allotments on our left, before opening out on to farmland. From here the walk is more attractive and, keeping to field paths and crossing two lanes, we reach the disused Lumpsey iron mine at (9).

We cross the rail line and then follow directions over grassland to the footbridge over Merry Lockwood Gill. There are now two field edges to follow as far as the track at (10). Here we go right for about 170m before turning left on the road and walking under two bridges into North Skelton.

Skelton Beck to the seafront at (4). This is certainly a more attractive route but is not designated CW and misses several treasure hunt clues.

If we take the road, we zigzag down the 1-in-4 old A174 road and continue eastwards over Skelton Beck.

Just after the toilets, the shorter walk forks right on the tarmac and then, a little further on, follows the footpath signposted to Saltburn Gill Nature Reserve. The longer walk forks left on the main

At the road bend immediately after St Peter's Church, we turn left on the Cleveland Street Walk and continue behind the houses and over Holme Beck to Stanghow Road (11). Turning right, we leave the CS and follow the road to the first turn left. Now we go up through Trout Hall Farm and on towards Skelton Green. But just before the houses, by a green metal seat, we take the track on our right (12) which will bend left and then continue to the tarmac CW path. Here we turn right between the fences and return to Skelton.

Special Interest – WALK 17

Saltburn Henry Pease is credited with deliberately setting out to make Saltburn the first planned seaside resort in England. After the railway was extended to Saltburn in 1861, he bought land from Lord Zetland to be developed as building plots and a new town developed to the west side of Skelton Beck. The Victorian fashion for spa water, together with the laying out of the Italian Gardens, helped to make the Valley Gardens attractive for visitors. The cliff railway, worked by an innovative system of water ballast, and the pier were further attractions. But look at the pier information board to see what a catalogue of mishaps and accidents the pier has suffered.

Rifts Wood lies in the sheltered **Saltburn Valley** believed to have been cut by meltwater at the end of the last Ice Age and now occupied by **Skelton Beck**. Marske Mill was once part of a complex of water mills along Skelton Beck but when the buildings were demolished in the 1960s only the stone foundations were left and there is little for us to see today. Rushpool Hall, now a hotel, is visible on the east side of the valley and is a neo-Gothic construction built originally for John Bell, the iron mine owner. Further down the valley lies the Albert Temple, originally the portico at Barnard Castle railway station but moved to Saltburn in 1867 following the death of Prince Albert. Sadly, it now stands forlorn and vandalised.

Saltburn Gill (not to be confused with Skelton Beck in Saltburn Valley) is the route for the short-circuit walk and this Nature Reserve is an SSSI and one of the few examples of semi-natural ancient woodland in East Cleveland. The valley is dominated by an oak-ash canopy and a mixed variety shrub layer. Bluebells and garlic abound in spring.

Smuggling 'Andrew's cow has calved' was the code for telling villagers that John Andrew's ship, the 'Morgan Rattler', had returned with a cargo of booty ready to be off-loaded. John Andrew, the so-called 'King of the Smugglers', had his headquarters at the Ship Inn and the Smugglers Heritage Centre next to the Inn recreates something of the exciting but dangerous 18th century atmosphere.

Hunt Cliff is one of three Wildlife Trust Nature Reserves found on this walk. The cliffs themselves ('a kittiwake city' according to one notice) support internationally important numbers of breeding kittiwakes and the grassland on top of the cliffs has a wide range of wildflowers including the regionally rare Dyer's Greenweed.

Hunt Cliff was the site of a Roman Signal Station but by 1911 half of the site had been eroded away by the sea. The remaining part was excavated before it, too, was lost to the waves. A line of stations existed along the coast between South Shields and Flamborough Head and these were designed to give early warning of sea-borne raids. The stations were probably built in AD 367 on the orders of Theodosius.

'New Milestones' is the title given to three modern steel sculptures made by Richard Farrington at the Skinningrove steelworks and on display along the CW above Hunt Cliff and next to Warsett Hill. Richard's sculptures reflect different aspects of life in East Cleveland. The large steel circle, for example, contains models of a Cleveland Bay Horse, Thor's hammer for metal working, a belemnite fossil, a mermaid's purse from the seashore and a cat (because cats were hunted here in the 1300s).

Skinningrove, previously a small fishing village, changed dramatically after the discovery of ironstone in 1848. Several mines were established in the locality and in 1874 an ironworks was set up. This was later expanded and in 1907 the works also began manufacturing steel. But in 1972 iron and steel production ceased and today the plant concentrates on making specialised items using steel from Teesside.

The **Tom Leonard Mining Museum** stands on the site of the old Loftus mine, the first of Cleveland's ironstone mines. It was a drift mine tunnelled into the side of the hill and the vertical shafts were used just for ventilation. Loftus became the third largest iron producer in Cleveland after Eston and Upleatham and continued to extract ironstone until 1958. The museum promises an exciting opportunity to experience something of the atmosphere of life underground as visitors are taken on a guided tour into the North Drift of the former mine.

Carlin How was a shaft mine working the Main Seam from 1873 and was commonly known as the 'Duck Hole' because water was constantly draining into the mine workings. This meant that from

This valley has been on the move – take a look, it's still moving today

1903 iron from Carlin How was brought to the surface through the Lumpsey Mine although the shaft was still used by the miners.

Cattersty Gill is a coastal valley supporting large tracts of hawthorn scrub. It is a winter resting and refuelling stop for migrant birds. This is a rare habitat along this coast - salty winds make tree growth difficult. Sheltered glades in the scrub are being preserved to provide habitat for insects and birds. Adjacent fields have been restored from the steelworks slag tippings.

Stone: Cleveland Coast stone, designed by Vivienne Mousdell, marking the beginning of the Heritage Coastline.

Special Interest – WALK 18

Alum production has been described as 'the first chemical industry' and we can see evidence of the quarrying and processing of alum-bearing rocks at a number of places along the coast. Though alum was also used for leather tanning and fire-proofing, its main use from the 14th century was as a mordant for fixing dyes in the textile industry. As England's main export to Europe was textiles, a supply of alum was extremely important but in the 15th and 16th centuries most of Europe's supply came from the Vatican and after Henry VIII broke relations with Rome, England needed to find an alternative source. Extraction first started at Slapewath in 1604 and quarries were developed on the Cleveland Escarpment and along the coast from Saltburn to Ravenscar.

Alum is a chemical containing aluminium sulphate and either ammonium or potassium sulphate. The process of converting suitable shale rocks into alum crystals was complicated, longwinded and, to modern eyes, highly polluting. Urine, to supply ammonium, was an important requirement.

Coastal location of the alum works allowed the transport of the crystals by sea and Whitby's developing shipbuilding industry helped to meet the increased demand for boats. The industry fell into decline when it was found that alum could be obtained more easily from coalfield waste and the last quarry ceased operation in 1871. Details of how the industry operated can be seen at the National Trust Centre at Ravenscar where we learn that it was widely believed the best urine to use came 'from the labouring people who take little strong drink'.

The Miners' Way is a walk of about six miles following paths formerly used by alum and ironstone miners. With a slight modification to include the Tom Leonard Museum and Skinningrove it forms one of the two short circuits which make up Walk 18.

Loftus used to be called 'Lofthouse' until the name was changed to avoid confusion with Lofthouse in West Yorkshire. Evidence of early occupation in the area is given by the excavations at Street House Farm which showed settlement dating back to Neolithic times. Records suggest that before the Norman Conquest of 1066 Loftus was a settlement of considerable importance but after the Rising of the North, King William's retaliation in 1069 laid waste to the region. Inhabitants were killed, livestock slaughtered and buildings destroyed. The Domesday Survey of 1086 valued the former farmland and woodland at nothing.

Loftus benefited greatly from the rise of the alum industry which became the main source of prosperity in the late 17th and 18th centuries. The houses at Foulsyke, Micklow and Upton were originally built for alum workers who were entitled by right to a cottage and the space to keep a cow.

Just as the alum industry was declining, ironstone was discovered locally. Ore from the Loftus mine was sent to the blast furnaces at Skinningrove for processing. The town's population was swelled by an influx of miners from other regions, notably from Cornwall where the copper mines were experiencing difficulties. Distinctly Cornish surnames in the locality today reflect this aspect of Loftus' history.

At the present time it is the extraction of another underground resource, potash at Boulby, which provides the region's mineral wealth.

St Leonard's Church in Loftus is located where a church has stood since before the Norman invasion but today's structure is the result of rebuilding in 1901. The churchyard contains the grave of Louis Hunton

who was born at Hummersea in 1814. Studying the cliffs near his home, he discovered how certain fossils, especially different ammonite species, were restricted to particular beds of rock. When he was only 22 years old, he wrote a classic paper showing how ammonites could be used as index fossils for identifying different rock strata. He died two years later.

The Newton Memorial Chapel was built in memory of Robert Newton of Roxby (1780-1854) who was four times President of the Wesleyan Conference. The chapel was demolished after damage by enemy action in the World War II.

Stone: Trig point (213m) above Rock Cliff, Boulby. Beneath its capping of boulder clay, the upper cliff is composed of the massive sandstones of the Ravenscar Group and below that lie the almost horizontal strata of the different rocks making up the Lias Group. More resistant layers of rock stand out as small ledges on the cliff face.

WALK 18
SKINNINGROVE –
BOULBY

Map: Explorer OL 27
S.E.P.: Skinningrove car park (713201)
Buses: X56, 65, M16
Cleveland Way distance: **2.6 miles**
Circular walk distance: **10.7 miles**
Shorter walk alternatives:
　　　　West loop　　　　**5.5 miles**
　　　　East loop　　　　**7.7 miles**
Special interest:
　　Alum working, Miners' Way, Loftus
Cross or Stone:
　　Trig point above Rock Cliff (750195)

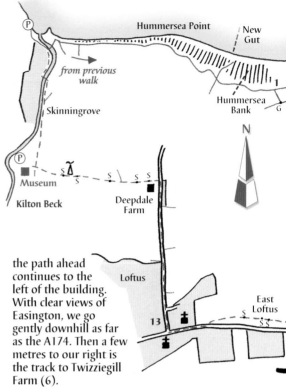

This walk includes the ascent of Rock Cliff, Boulby, the highest cliff on the east coast of England (203m according to the National Trail guide; 213m at the nearby trig point) followed by a loop around Easington before returning to Skinningrove via Loy Lane and Loftus. Suitable starts are from the sea-front car park at Skinningrove or by the Tom Leonard Museum. The Miners' Way can be used to create a shorter circuit.

Setting off from the seafront car park at Skinningrove, we walk along Marine Terrace, cross Kilton Beck and climb the steep, stone-stepped path of the CW. We now have a stretch of bracing cliff-top walking. After we pass Hummersea Point we see, when the tide is out, the extensive rocky wave-cut platform with the New Gut channel that was cut into the rock to allow ships to approach the alum refinery. The CW turns inland at (1) and then as we enter a second N.T. property (2) we can soon view the remains of the Loftus alum quarry which was the largest in Britain and provided the raw material for the refinery at Hummersea.

At (3) the Miners' Way leads off right and this route forms the shorter walk. The longer walk continues to the information board at (4) and we should certainly spend a few minutes reading about the details of alum processing; Londoners, we find, played a pivotal role in aiding Cleveland's early industrial development. But there was no such thing as an Environmental Impact Assessment in those days and patches of orange alum spoil are still visible.

At (5) we turn right to the trig point (213m) marking the highest cliff in eastern England and here readers of ECHOES (or Eckoes) should remember to pay appropriate homage. We carry on to the telecommunications mast from where

the path ahead continues to the left of the building. With clear views of Easington, we go gently downhill as far as the A174. Then a few metres to our right is the track to Twizziegill Farm (6).

We have to turn left immediately before the farm and at the end of the buildings, the p.r.o.w. goes across arable land. However, a 'request route' waymarks us right and then left along the sides of the field to (7). From here we carry on down to the rail line.

Crossing with care, we follow the narrow path bearing left and then down through Mines Wood with its numerous dead trees lying decaying on the floor, across an open area by the former mine, then up very steeply through the trees again to the stile at (8). From here we are led over a field to East Ridge Farm visible on Ridge Lane.

We turn right and walk along Ridge Lane. It's not busy and I don't recommend turning off to use the path on the right at (9) – it's narrow and slippery – but instead I prefer to continue to the next signposted p.r.o.w. crossing at (10). This is about 350m after the first 'SLOW' sign painted on the road. Turning right, the path takes us down to and across Easington Beck, where we veer slightly left and then follow the waymarks up to Spring House Cottages.

Going through the small gate to the left of the cottages, we

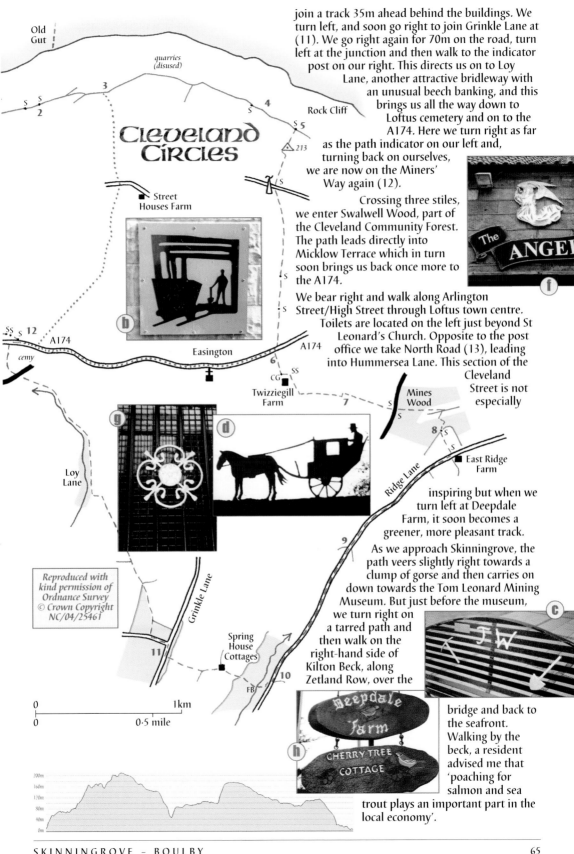

join a track 35m ahead behind the buildings. We turn left, and soon go right to join Grinkle Lane at (11). We go right again for 70m on the road, turn left at the junction and then walk to the indicator post on our right. This directs us on to Loy Lane, another attractive bridleway with an unusual beech banking, and this brings us all the way down to Loftus cemetery and on to the A174. Here we turn right as far as the path indicator on our left and, turning back on ourselves, we are now on the Miners' Way again (12).

Crossing three stiles, we enter Swalwell Wood, part of the Cleveland Community Forest. The path leads directly into Micklow Terrace which in turn soon brings us back once more to the A174.

We bear right and walk along Arlington Street/High Street through Loftus town centre. Toilets are located on the left just beyond St Leonard's Church. Opposite to the post office we take North Road (13), leading into Hummersea Lane. This section of the Cleveland Street is not especially inspiring but when we turn left at Deepdale Farm, it soon becomes a greener, more pleasant track.

As we approach Skinningrove, the path veers slightly right towards a clump of gorse and then carries on down towards the Tom Leonard Mining Museum. But just before the museum, we turn right on a tarred path and then walk on the right-hand side of Kilton Beck, along Zetland Row, over the bridge and back to the seafront. Walking by the beck, a resident advised me that 'poaching for salmon and sea trout plays an important part in the local economy'.

Old Gut

quarries (disused)

Cleveland Circles

Rock Cliff

213

Street Houses Farm

b

A174   12

cemy

Easington   A174   6

Twizziegill Farm   CG   SS   7   Mines Wood   8   East Ridge Farm

Ridge Lane

Loy Lane   g   d   c   9

Reproduced with kind permission of Ordnance Survey © Crown Copyright NC/04/25461

Grinkle Lane

Spring House Cottages   11   10   FB

Deepdale Farm   CHERRY TREE COTTAGE   h

The ANGEL   f

0   1km
0   0·5 mile

200m
160m
120m
80m
40m
0m

WALK 19
BOULBY –
RUNSWICK BANK TOP

(DOG LOUP)

Map: Explorer OL 27
S.E.P.T.: Runswick Bank Top car park (808161)
Buses: X56, 65, M16
Cleveland Way distance: **5.4 miles**
Circular walk distance: **11.4 miles**
Shorter walk alternatives:
    West loop   **6.1 miles**
    East loop   **6.9 miles**
Special interest:
    Boulby Mine, Staithes, Port Mulgrave
Cross or Stone: War Memorial (795165)

the Port Mulgrave road sign to see St Hilda's Well in St Hilda's Churchyard.

Then we retrace our steps, cross over the A174 and go down West End Close to Porrett Lane. Turning right, the road soon becomes a track and swings round left before coming to the red-coloured house at (1). A sharp right turn leads us over two stiles and then we descend into the trees beside Dales Beck. Crossing the footbridge, we rise steeply up the steps. On leaving the trees the way over the field is not obvious but the p.r.o.w. leads off at 11.00 o'clock direction to the stile at the edge of Oakrigg Wood (2).

Following the waymark directing us right just inside the trees, we take a very attractive path through mixed deciduous woodland. Then entering Oak Ridge Nature Reserve, we soon come to the gate at (3) from where the woodland opens out and fresh planting among the bracken and scrub has taken place.

As we leave the Reserve we come to the bridge at (4) where several paths converge. We take the track on the right hand side of the main stream leading NW and signposted to Dalehouse.

This walk takes us along the cliff-top CW from Boulby through Cowbar-Staithes and Port Mulgrave to Runswick Bank Top. The circuit is completed through Hinderwell, Dalehouse and several wooded valleys. Convenient links allow the full, longer walk to be divided into 2, 3 or 4 shorter circuits if desired.

Runswick Bank Top car park has public toilets, so the full circuit starts from here and we walk clockwise on the non-Cleveland Way section first and then finish the walk along the cliff-top.

From Runswick Bank Top we use the pavement alongside Hinderwell Lane to Hinderwell village where we turn right on the A174 road. We go to the end of the village and turn off right at

The young James Cook received his first taste of the sea and ships in this harbour village, where he worked as an assistant to William Sanderson, merchant, for 18 months from 1745.

A right turn at Dalehouse (5) takes the short walk back to Staithes but the longer route goes left over the bridge and then immediately right following another stream along Ridge Lane.

Just after the ford a bridleway goes right to Boulby but we bend left and stay on Ridge Lane for about 120m until we come to the p.r.o.w. on our right (6). We branch off here to take a wide track through the trees. At (7) there is an eerie view through the long disused rail tunnel on our left but we turn sharp right over Easington Beck and then immediately left. We avoid the first track going up right towards Boulby Mine and continue ahead across the open area marking the site of an old mine.

Soon we reach the path junction (8) that was crossed on Walk 18. We turn right at the picnic table and climb up through Mines Wood to the rail track. After crossing the railway, we turn sharp right and walk along the field edge parallel to the rail line and down to another small wooded valley. Veering left to the old red brick machinery

building, we use the stile just beyond the far side of the building to lead us down to the confluence of two small streams. Crossing both streams, we pick up a narrow, little-used, path to the right of the beck that is on the right. Staying close to the water, this leads us up through Newton Gill Wood. When we emerge at the steps we follow the fence on our left and go alongside two fields and through a patch of scrub before reaching the A174 at (9).

After crossing the road we take the path to the left of Ings Farm Holiday Cottages. It may be a little overgrown but we keep going straight ahead and then at (10) waymarks direct us round to the road at Boulby Barns Farm. We turn left along the road, then right at the telecommunications mast and, passing the trig point, join the CW at the stile (11).

Navigation along the coast for the next five miles is easy but we need to be aware of possible cliff slips and gusts of wind where the path runs particularly close to the cliff edge. Shortly after passing Boulby, we approach Cowbar along a metalled road and we could spend a few minutes admiring the view from the top of Cow Bar Nab before descending steeply to Staithes on the other side of Staithes Beck.

Leaving Staithes, we go up Church Street past Captain Cook's Cottage, Dog Loup and St Peter's Church before bearing left up the stone-stepped CW path. Where the land flattens out the route can become muddy but our direction up and round the side of Beacon Hill is obvious and we soon arrive at Port Mulgrave.

Before we turn left off the road we can consult the information board (12) which gives fascinating detail about Port Mulgrave's former function as an ironstone shipment port. Then we continue round Lingrow Cliffs to (13) where the CW acorn directs us right and back to Runswick Bank Top.

Special Interest – WALK 19

Boulby Mine is one of the world's major **potash** producers. The rock occurs at depths of between 1200 and 1500 metres in a seam averaging about 7 metres in thickness. As well as producing potash for use as fertiliser, the mine also recovers, as a by-product, salt which is used mostly for road de-icing. Some of the potash is exported from Teesside.

The Boulby Mine is also important for another, quite different, reason. It is a centre for astronomical research. Astronomers have known for some time that there is a lot more matter in the universe than can be seen in the light of stars like our sun. This extra matter that we cannot see is known as 'dark matter'. One idea is that the dark matter consists of **WIMPS** – Weakly Interactive Massive Particles. These are subatomic particles that are predicted by a recent (as yet unproven) theory of particle physics. They have to be massive because their gravitational attraction is important. It is also clear that they interact very weakly with matter as they haven't yet been detected. Several experiments are in progress and are still being developed in the Boulby mine to try and detect these WIMPS for the first time. The experiments have to be at a sufficient depth to shield out cosmic rays – subatomic particles that reach us from space and which would interfere with the detection of WIMPS. Boulby mine is one of the deepest mines in the country and so has been chosen as the site for these experiments. I am grateful to Professor Peter Main for this information.

Staithes To those who know it well, Staithes remains an endearing spot. It contains what is claimed to be the narrowest street in Yorkshire – Dog Loup – and the CW passes by it.

'Staithe' indicates a landing place and the village is one of the few reasonably safe harbours along the Heritage Coast. For centuries Staithes relied on the sea for its livelihood and a couple of hundred years ago it was the largest fishing port on the east coast north of the Wash. There were 70 cobles and 14 'five-man boats' (crewed by seven men and boys). Large hauls of herring were caught in summer as the shoals moved down the coast from Scotland. Line fishing was

also carried out – one line having as many as 300 individually baited hooks. Johnny Cole's workshop was one of the boat-building enterprises concentrated along the Beckside and adjacent to them was a row of fish curing houses.

The arrival of rail transport which allowed the rapid movement of fresh fish meant the curing industry became obsolete, while the development of large, iron-built, steam-driven trawlers forced many of the smaller boats at Staithes out of business.

The Staithes area is known to have been occupied over a long period of prehistory. Mesolithic flint tools have been found near Loftus and at Street House both Neolithic as well as Bronze Age burial sites have been excavated. Jet buttons unearthed at one burial mound remind us that Queen Victoria was not the first person to make these black ornaments fashionable. But what has excited archaeologists in recent years has been the discovery in 2001 of a Bronze Age timber structure at Staithes. Waterlogged timbers had been noticed in the bank of Staithes Beck and it was thought that these might have been related to 17th century coastal trade when industrial developments associated with alum processing began. However, radiocarbon dating of the timbers produced astonishing results: the wood, still with bark covering, dated back to the early Bronze Age. Possible interpretations suggest there may have been some sort of jetty or even a weir at the site.

Several Iron Age hill-fort sites have already been observed on Cleveland Circles walks and there is some evidence that Cowbar Nab may also have been a promontory fort of this age, defended by a dyke on its landward side and steep cliffs facing the sea.

Staithes lies on the Captain Cook Trail because in 1745 James Cook came to Staithes to work for William Sanderson in his grocer's shop. The shop was destroyed by the sea but parts were rebuilt into 'Cook's Cottage' which we pass in Church Street. The Heritage Centre in High Street relates part of the Cook saga.

Port Mulgrave in the 19th century was an important centre for the extraction and movement of iron ore. Trucks ran out of the mine entrance (now blocked up) on to a gantry and the ironstone was tipped into bunkers for storage before being shipped up the coast to Jarrow.

Workers from Lincolnshire and Norfolk supplemented the local labour force and their cottages, each with its own pigsty, were of a distinctly better standard than was usual at the time. The local mine had only a short life but when a new mine was opened at Grinkle Park about three miles away the ironstone was

Boulby Mine

brought through tunnels to the harbour at Port Mulgrave. The harbour was used by the mine until 1917 when the mine became linked to Middlesbrough by rail.

Cross or Stone: Hinderwell War Memorial stands at the junction of the A174 and Hinderwell Lane.

Special Interest – WALK 20

The village of **Runswick Bay** was originally located to the north of Lingrow Beck but in 1664 a huge landslip caused the settlement to slide into the sea. By morning only one house was still standing – that of the dead man whose wake the villagers had been observing the night before. The village was rebuilt but the steeply sloping land has continued to suffer from slippage.

For centuries fishing was the mainstay of the village economy and the August herring catch was regularly taken down to Yarmouth for sale but regular fishing had come to an end by 1950. Smuggling, of course, used to supplement the income and the Fox Inn at Roxby was allegedly an important contraband collecting point.

Most fishing villages have their own special tales of lifeboat heroism. Perhaps Runswick's most famous was the 1901 action when most of the regular lifeboat crew were already out at sea fishing. It was left to the women and old men to launch the boat and 'stand by' until the cobles returned safely.

A stroll around the village will enable us to identify the sites of a number of interesting structures: the former village bakery next to Ebor House, the Methodist Chapel built in 1829 by the women of the village and the old Paraffin House where Sea Cliffe now stands.

Kettleness, like Runswick Bay, has suffered from cliff collapse. In 1829 a massive landslip caused the settlement to slump into the sea and the villagers had to be rescued by a ship standing offshore.

Goldsborough was the site of one of the Roman signal stations built along the coast between Hunt Cliff and Filey.

Wade's Stone(s): There are two stones with this name; we see one on this walk but the other is found close to the Outdoor Centre at East Barnby. Various tales are told about the legendary giant Wade and these stories may be based on a Saxon Duke Wada who lived at Lythe.

WALK 20
RUNSWICK BANK TOP
– TELLGREEN HILL

Map: Explorer OL 27
S.E.P.T.: Runswick Bank Top car park
(808161)
Buses: X56, 65, M16
Cleveland Way distance: **4.0 miles**
Circular walk distance: **8.8 miles**
Shorter walk alternatives:
West loop **4.6 miles**
East loop **5.8 miles**
Special interest:
Runswick Bay
Cross or Stone: Wade's Stone (829144)

The long itinerary for this walk extends along the Cleveland Way from Runswick Bank Top to Tellgreen Hill, returning via Goldsborough and a stretch of disused rail track. There is a variety of cliff scenery and undulating farmland. The path inland from High Cliff allows the main circuit to be split into two shorter walks. Some groups may wish to continue along the coast from Tellgreen Hill to Sandsend. This will save mileage on the following walk, which runs from Sandsend to Whitby, as well as allowing more time to explore Whitby. It is advisable to check tide times for crossing Runswick Sands.

We start from the upper car park, with its toilet facilities, at Runswick Bank Top. The O.S. map shows the CW using the new road from the car park down to Runswick Sands; fingerposts on the ground still show the route on the old road. Assuming we follow the fingerposts and the old road, we zigzag down to the beach but a quick detour to explore the village is highly recommended before we strike off across the sands (1).

Assuming the tide is out, we can walk on the sandy beach before observing the notice (near the sailing club hut) advising us that the CW goes up the next gulley. The 'Hob Holes' we see at the foot of the cliff face are the remains of jet mines that have been further eroded by the sea.

When we turn off at the waymark at Claymoor Beck (2) we go up into a spectacular little gorge with steps cut, firstly, in the shale rock and then, on the other side of the stream, into the soil. At the top of the steps, we have the customary excuse of

looking back at the view whilst we stop for a breather.

We carry on along the cliff top and then at the first field boundary (3) a p.r.o.w. heads off diagonally right up High Cliff and this path affords a short circuit route via Barnby Tofts back to Runswick Bay.

As we continue on the longer route we pass alongside the line of a dismantled railway and a few stiles later we come to Kettleness. Waymark indicators direct us round the outside of Kettleness Farm and then the CW forks off left from the tarred road.

There are interesting views down to the desolate area of disused quarries on Kettle Ness but, on this occasion, no information board. However, this is the place famous for its fossils of huge marine reptiles and as recently as 1999 a complete ichthyosaur skeleton was found here. Swinging round the headland we are reminded from the O.S. map that there was once a Roman Signal Station at Goldsborough.

We continue above Ovalgate Cliff to the p.r.o.w. signposted to Lythe (4). Going right and then right again at the next field boundary, we soon join with the bridleway coming up from Overdale Farm. Continuing westwards on a broad firm track, we arrive in Goldsborough. (Note: the pub is likely to be closed in winter.)

In the village we turn left on the road to East and West Barnby and look for the second footpath leading off right and signed for Brockrigg Farm (5). A few hundred metres along this stony track we spot the Wade's Stone near the edge of the field on our left.

Shortly after Brockrigg Farm we should go carefully because the waymark (between the 3rd and 4th cattle grids) indicating the path leading off left (6) may be hidden in tall grass. The path goes down, then up, to Barnby Tofts. The p.r.o.w. turns right just before the farm and then goes due west following field boundaries. The views ahead of rolling green farmland make an unexpected contrast with the cliff scenery we saw earlier on the walk.

We go past a small patch of trees on our left but, about 200m further on, the path cutting down diagonally right (7) may not be clear. Aiming for Runswick Bank Top, the legal p.r.o.w. goes over the stream at the bottom of the slope and then up towards Westfields Farm before doubling back to the gate above the dismantled rail line. However, the farmer generously allows walkers to continue to the next stream a short way ahead and then to follow the hedge down to the field corner (8) and use the gate there in order to gain access to the disused rail track. (Please remember that this helpful gesture in no way whatsoever confers any general right of public access.) Turning left on the former rail track we walk for a little over a mile on a pleasant, hedge-lined trail that must bear little resemblance to its former industrial appearance. The track narrows to a path shortly before we come to Ellerby Lane (9) where we turn right and return to Runswick Bank Top.

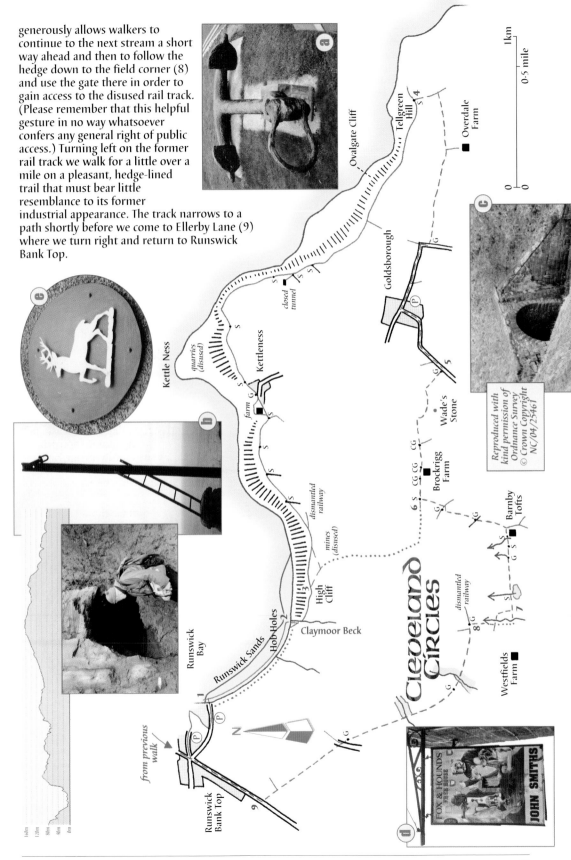

Reproduced with kind permission of Ordnance Survey © Crown Copyright NC/04/25461

Cleveland Circles

from previous walk

This is a figure-of-eight walk centred on Sandsend and consists of a 'Lythe Loop' and a 'Whitby Loop'. Tide times should be checked beforehand so that the Sandsend to Whitby stretch can be walked on the sand rather than along the main A174 road.

WALK 21
TELLGREEN HILL
– WHITBY

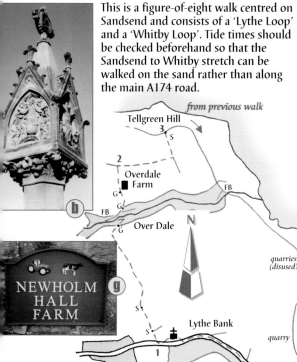

Map: Explorer OL 27
S.E.P.T.: Sandsend car park (860129)
Buses: X56, 65, M16
Cleveland Way distance: **4.7 miles**
Circular walk distance: **11.6 miles**
Shorter walk alternatives:
      Lythe loop   **3.6 miles**
      West Whitby loop   **8.0 miles**
Special interest:
    Whitby Town Trail (west side), Mulgrave
    Woods, Sneaton Castle, Sandsend Trail
Cross: Stakesby Cross (885110)

Cement' Mill by the car park. Then, depending on the state of the tide, we may be able to use the beach as we continue to Whitby, otherwise we will need to take the road. If we do walk on the sand, we come up after a mile or so on to the concrete promenade (5) built as part of the town's sea defences and cliff stabilisation work. We continue through the archway of the red-bricked Whitby Pavilion and then just a short way further on we come to the Captain Cook memorial overlooking the harbour – plenty of opportunities for photo experimentation.

Starting from Sandsend car park, with its toilets, we turn right and walk on the pavement by the A174 up the steep 25% gradient of Lythe Bank to St Oswald's Church. Looking back, we get stunning views of Whitby. A look round the church can be used as a justifiable excuse to regain breath and we should not leave until we have at least found the two ophicleides.

Just past the church we turn right (1) on to a pleasant bridleway which takes us into the valley of Over Dale. Part of the path includes a paved trod and then after crossing the beck the path rises and turns left at the kissing gate to bring us up to and through Overdale Farm.

A little way beyond the farm we join the p.r.o.w. used on Walk 20 (2). This time we turn right, then left and come back to the CW (3).

Turning right, the CW comes inland slightly before the steep drop into Over Dale. Steps make the descent easier and when we reach the flat course of the former railway (the blocked tunnel is just to our right) we bear left and follow the track past the remains of the Deep Grove Quarries. This brings us back to the car park at Sandsend. Marker posts along the track indicate points on the Sandsend Trail, details of which are available from the T.I.C.

We follow the A174 round Sandsend to East Row (4) and take a quick look at the old 'Roman

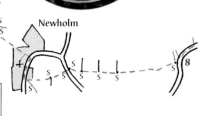

Reproduced with kind permission of Ordnance Survey © Crown Copyright NC/04/25461

0   1km
0   0·5 mile

The O.S. map shows the CW turning right on the road but we may take a short cut and use the path going steeply down in front of us to meet the 'Khyber Pass' road. Here we turn left and keep going down to the waterside. Now we turn right along Pier Road. Here are all manner of temptations to make you dawdle; we may resist the amusement arcades but are we strong-willed enough to pass the fudge factory?

When we reach the bridge over the Esk (6) we turn sharp right by the Nat West Bank, taking the steep narrow road up past the Golden Lion. We bend left into Flowergate, continue up past the Archives & Heritage Centre, and come to St Hilda's Terrace with the Whitby Museum and Pannett Art Gallery ahead on our left.

At the roundabout (7) we go down Spring Vale which runs into Stakesby Road and then after we have bent round left along Castle Road we take the right fork along the B1460. Sneaton Castle is ahead on our left.

Leaving suburbia, we continue up round the bend in the road and go over the stile on our right (8). We now follow field edges and cross another seven waymarked stiles (and one road) into Newholm. We turn right, then just after Ye Olde Beehive pub, we go left down Howlgate Lane. After nearly 300m the path leads off right (9) over a stile, just before the caravans. We then branch left after 40m or so down

into the trees to follow a small beck. Crossing a footbridge, we climb up steps and come to a fingerpost along the field edge (10) directing us left to Dunsley.

We go as far as the next field boundary, turning right to yet another attractive stream. After crossing the footbridge and stile we head over the field to the farm on the skyline; the approach may be muddied with cattle trampling.

A right turn takes us through Dunsley before we go right again at the road T-junction (11). Care is then needed not to miss the indicator post further along the lane (12) - it's about 120m after the farm track off left. From (12) four stiles and a gate lead us across farmland in the general direction of the tall disused water tower.

Just after the gate we go down into our last delightful wooded valley and before long come out at the wide track taking us back to East Row. We go right, then left over the bridge, to return to our start at Sandsend.

Olde Beehive Inne
We in this hive are all alive,
good liquor makes our money.
If you are dry come in, and try
the flavour of our honey.

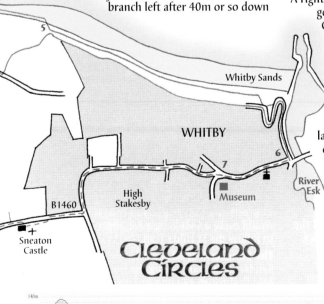

Whitby Sands

WHITBY

High Stakesby

B1460

Sneaton Castle

Museum

River Esk

Cleveland Circles

1774
REMEMBER THY END

140m
100m
60m
20m

Special Interest – WALK 21

Whitby's Seafaring Traditions It is reported that at one time Whitby was the sixth largest port in Britain and the third biggest shipbuilding centre in the country. Fishburn's shipyard was one of a number of yards once located on the banks of the River Esk. Here a great variety of ships was built including the 'Endeavour', 'Resolution', and 'Adventure' used by James Cook on his three voyages of discovery. These ships were colliers, designed originally for transporting coal, and with their flat bottoms and shallow draft were, if necessary, relatively easy to refloat. James Cook came to Whitby in 1746 as an apprentice to John Walker, the ship-owner.

During the height of its whaling prosperity (1753-1833) a total of 2,761 whales were landed at Whitby. The oil was especially prized but almost all the other parts of the whale had a use. It hardly needs saying, but harpooning whales was a hazardous venture. The Scoresbys, Senior and Junior, were inventors and Arctic explorers as well as whaling captains. William (Senior) invented the barrel crow's nest while his son is remembered for his experiments to improve the magnetic compass. The whalebones which form the arch by the Cook monument came from Alaska in 2002 and replace an earlier pair.

One of the perils of living in a prosperous seaport was that you were liable to be pressganged into the marine service. In 1795, parliament passed two Acts forcing counties to provide a quota of men for the Royal Navy. Yorkshire had to provide over 1,000 men and the port of Whitby was an obvious recruiting place. Whaling crews were supposed to be exempt from the enforced conscription but in reality there was little protection against the thuggery of the licensed pressgangs.

Today the port of Whitby acts mainly as a fishing harbour but since the construction of the

Endeavour Wharf in 1964 there has been some increase in cargo trade. The reclaimed area also provides berths for numerous pleasure craft.

Mulgrave Woods have two 'proper' castles and a third castellated house that is known as a castle. The oldest is at the site of Lythe Castle (Foss Mill) on a cliff above Barnby Beck. It was a motte and bailey wooden structure and is thought to have been built by Nigel Fossard. The remains are marked on the O.S. map as 'Motte' (832117). That earlier building was replaced in 1214 by 'Old' Mulgrave Castle (839117) but the structure today is considered to be dangerous and cannot be examined too closely. The Parliamentarians ordered it to be made untenable after the Civil War and it has been in ruins since then. 'New' Mulgrave Castle (847126) is the fine house started by the Buckingham family before 1735, although converting the house into a 'castle' with battlements was carried out later. The grounds were planned by Capability Brown and here Charles Dickens is said to have danced the hornpipe on the terrace known as the Quarterdeck. In the mid-1800s the Maharajah Dhuleep Singh lived at the castle. Prompted, so the story goes, by the fact that his elephants didn't like getting sand between their toes, the Maharajah paid for the construction of a road between Whitby and Sandsend. Mulgrave Woods are open to the public on Wednesdays, Saturdays and Sundays (but not in May).

The battlemented structure known as **Sneaton Castle** has had a varied history. It started in about 1813 as Claremont Lodge when James Holloway had a plan to provide education for 'young Gentlemen'. This project failed and a new owner, Colonel James Wilson, converted the Lodge in the 1820s into a building that was designed to resemble the ancient castle of Sneaton. This castle no longer existed but an old woodcut picture gave a good idea of its appearance. During the rest of the 19th century the property was leased to various people but then in 1915 the Sisters of the Order of the Holy Paraclete, an Anglican religious community, came to occupy the castle and use it as a girls' boarding school. They were responsible for numerous alterations and additions to the school and chapel. However, the school had to close in 1997 and the buildings have been modified into the Sneaton Castle Centre that now acts as a conference and retreat centre. It would make an ideal base for anyone planning to follow the St Hilda Trail (see Walk 22).

The Sandsend Trail is a 2.5 mile walk from Sandsend car park, along the track of the old Middlesbrough rail line and on concessionary paths in the Mulgrave Estate. It passes the sites of three former alum quarries as well as the location of two cementstone mines. The alum

shales were processed at the Alum House, which was where the car park is today, and the cement shales were processed into 'Roman cement' at East Row. Roman cement is a hydraulic cement that sets under water and so was important for building sea walls and piers. Hard nodules (called 'doggers') were found in the alum shales and on the beach and they were crushed to make the cement at East Row where the complete plant has survived, a survival unique in the country.

Stakesby Cross at the junction of Stakesby Road with Love Lane is a restoration of a Mile Cross of Whitby Abbey put in place as part of the 1951 Festival of Britain celebrations.

Whitby Abbey – WALK 22

Whitby Abbey with its magnificent location on top of East Cliff is one of Yorkshire's most impressive landmarks. The original Abbey of Streoneshalh is believed to have been on Abbey Plain and was founded by Oswy, King of Northumbria, to commemorate his victory in 655 over Penda, the pagan king of Mercia. In 867 this first abbey was destroyed by Danish invaders but around 1076 a new abbey was built by Reinfrid for monks of the Benedictine Order. However most of the abbey buildings we see today were constructed in the 12th and 13th centuries.

When Henry VIII dissolved the monastery in 1539, the abbey was stripped of its lead, glass and other valuables and the abbey lands were sold to the Cholmley family. Over the next few centuries, the buildings became derelict, local people carried off the stone for their own purposes, storm damage caused further deterioration of the structure and then in 1914 German warships shelling the Yorkshire coast hit the west front of the abbey.

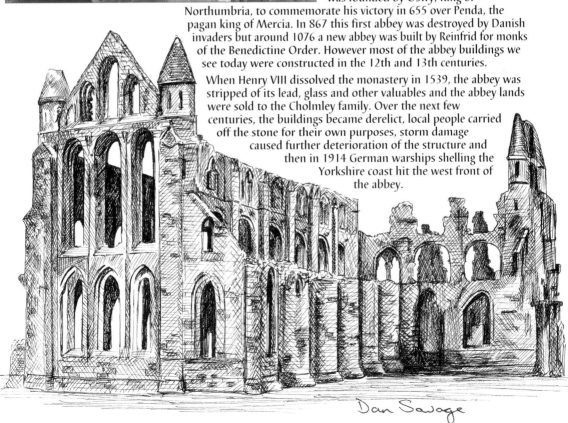

Dan Savage

WALK 22
WHITBY –
near HAWSKER

Map: Explorer OL 27
S.E.P.T.: Whitby (900106). Parking also
         at Hawsker, Sneaton or Ruswarp
Buses: X56, 65, M16, X40, 93, 93A, 99
         Rail to Whitby
Cleveland Way distance: **3.6 miles**
Circular walk distance: **10.9 miles**
Shorter walk alternatives:
      North loop   **7.5 miles**
      South-west loop   **7.3 miles**
      South-east loop   **5.3 miles**
Special interest:
   Whitby Abbey, Whitby Town Trail (east)
Crosses: Caedmon Cross (901112), Abbey
       Cross (902113), Caedmon Replica
       Cross (897101)

This walk includes the cliff scenery of the CW, some delightful woodland, rolling farmland, an ancient Monk's paved way as well as the spectacularly situated Whitby Abbey.

Assuming we start from the Langborne Road car park in Whitby (1) we walk north to the swing bridge over the River Esk to the point reached on Walk 21. We cross the river and immediately over the bridge take a quick look at the Cook Museum down Grape Lane. Then we continue along Sandgate before going right into the old Market Place, past the old Town Hall, and then left on to Church Street.

Church Street with its great variety of craft and tourist shops leads us to the famous 199 steps which take us up towards St Mary's Church and Whitby Abbey.

The CW swings round the outside of the Abbey grounds (note the ancient Abbey Cross on the left) before turning sharp left (2) at Abbey Farm to reach the cliff edge. From here we turn right and follow the CW for three miles. Our route is obvious though we should be prepared for minor deviations from the established path because of cliff slumping. We walk through the Whitby Holiday Park caravan site and then leave the tarred driveway at the stile (3). Black Nab appears ahead of us like a submarine emerging from the water.

We pass Whitby Fog Signal Station and then are soon directed around the nearby lighthouse before climbing the steps up to High Whitby. A short distance ahead is the path going off right for the short walk route (4) and then about 1100m further on after that, by the memorial seat (5), the long walk turns inland for Hawsker. The path follows the field edge then crosses to the gate at Gnipe Howe Farm. Here we turn left and a wide bridleway takes us into High Hawsker. We turn right on the road and soon come to the alternative

parking place on the A171 at (6). Crossing carefully, we bend left down Mill Lane and walk through Low Hawsker. On our right we see the shaft remains of Hawsker Cross.

At the end of the village where the road bends left by the waste water plant, we take the stile on our right (7). We descend, cross the footbridge and come up to a cultivated field. The waymark may be missing but we cross at 11.00 o'clock direction to another stile roughly halfway along the opposite field boundary. This leads us down to another attractive stream, Intake Beck, and the path then brings us up to the stile at (8). From here the field-side path to Stainsacre Lane should be drier!

The shorter S.W. and S.E. circuits turn right along Stainsacre Lane; the longer

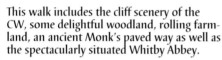

Cleveland Circles

ARGUMENTS YARD

D.
M :S
16.88.

0   1km
0   0·5 mile

Reproduced with kind permission of Ordnance Survey © Crown Copyright NC/04/25461

walk goes left on the lane for 60m before turning right towards The Riggs. A tarred route now takes us down to Rigg Mill but we must turn off right just before the ford in order to use the footbridge over Rigg Mill Beck. In springtime this is a lovely spot and, indeed, the next half-mile following the beck through the wood is delightful. When the track soon forks, we stay right and then, where we meet the path coming in on our right over the footbridge, we bend up left (9). Be prepared; the next few hundred metres may be muddy.

(10) but before venturing down the ancient flagged Monks' Walk we should have a look inside St Hilda's Church a little further along the road.

We continue down Monk's Walk. Although we cannot be sure that this ancient trod was originally paved by the monks (the stone slabs may have been laid at a later date) it is assumed that this is undoubtedly a route used at one time by Whitby Abbey.

As we reach yet another pretty stream, Shawn Riggs Beck, large 'bridgestones' make crossing easier but soon the flagstones become covered as the muddy path carries on over Shawn Riggs. We cross the road going to Golden Grove and then continue down on the trod to the footbridge at the confluence of Stainsacre Beck and Rigg Mill Beck (11). Turning left over the bridge and walking to the hairpin road bend at (12) we bear left and continue into Ruswarp.

At the junction (13) we turn right over the River Esk and the rail line, pass St Bartholomew's Church on our left and then, 20m past the post office, go right at the flagged footpath signposted to Whitby. This leads us round to the steps at (14). By the seat just beyond the top of the steps we take the path forking right. We then soon go down steps and over a disused rail track and almost immediately cross another track, before coming to Caedmon School's sport field. Here Esk Valley leaping salmon indicators show our route across the grass between the long jump pit and the football pitches. Then we bend left along the edge of the school car park and reach the A171 again (15).

Turning right for about 70m on the path next to the security fencing, we use the underpass beneath the road and follow the path going down to the houses at Waterstead Lane. Going ahead for 40m, we take the track bearing slightly right, cross the rail line and walk beside the River Esk into Whitby.

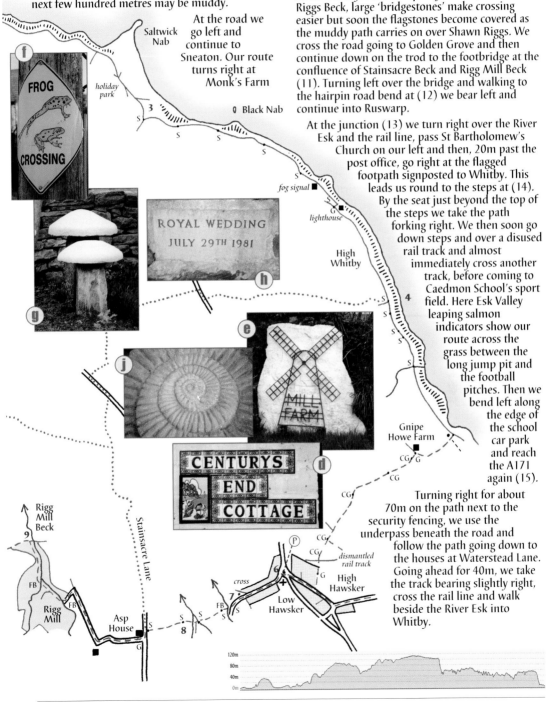

Special Interest – WALK 22

Whitby Town Trail (east side) Whitby's Market Place was laid out in 1640 when the site was moved from its old position at the western end of the river bridge, though the Town Hall was built much later. It can't have been a pleasant place in the 17th century because it was here that huge vats of stale urine were stored for use in the alum making industry. But apparently the smell of urine was nowhere near as bad as the stench of boiling whale blubber after the whaling ships returned with their cargoes. It was so awful that it's said grown men could be made to weep.

Church Street is a stroller's delight; but a nightmare for goods traffic. At one time, at least 20 of its houses were pubs. Along here many of the shops selling jet jewellery were found and at the end of the street is the Jet Heritage Centre. It is a working example of a Victorian jet workshop that was relocated here after being discovered sealed in an old attic elsewhere in the town. Leading down from Church Street to the riverside are the 'yards' and 'ghauts' with their tightly packed old cottages. In fact, there are 188 buildings listed as being of national importance along Church Street and in its yards. On Henrietta Street kippers are still cured in the traditional way with oak chippings.

St Mary's Church probably stands on or near the site of the Church of St Peter which was linked to the monastery built by King Oswy.

A detailed history of the church is available from the information desk but one thing we should not miss is the memorial stone to Francis and Mary Huntrodd, born on the same day, married on their birthday and who died within five hours of each other on their birthday in 1680.

The St Hilda Trail is a 101-mile long car trail visiting 14 churches in the region that have dedications to, or links with, St Hilda. A number of these are visited on, or lie close to, Cleveland Circles walks. As well as Whitby Abbey and three churches in Whitby, these include churches at Sneaton Castle (Walk 21), Sneaton village (Walk 22), Bilsdale (Walk 11), Liverton Mines (Walks 17, 18), and Hinderwell (Walk 19).

St Hilda was an exceptional figure in the history of English Christianity. She was a relative of King Edwin of Northumbria and grew up in his household. When he became a Christian in 627 she also was baptised. Bede tells us that Hilda's life fell into two equal parts. Until she was 33, she lived the regular life of a noblewoman. Then she decided to adopt the religious life. Aidan persuaded her to stay in Northumbria and after leading a small monastery at Hartlepool she became founding abbess of the new monastery at Steoneshalh (Whitby). Hilda was the superior of both monks and nuns and was responsible for the management of a large estate with many labourers and craftsmen. The monastery had to be self-sufficient and would not employ serfs, though they were still to be commonly found in England in the seventh century.

Hilda built up a library of manuscripts and became the principal of what was virtually a theological college. It was she who encouraged the herdsman Caedmon to develop his talent for composing sacred poems and songs.

In 664 Abbess Hilda presided over the momentous Synod of Whitby. This sought to resolve the differences between the practices of the northern, Celtic Church and the southern, Roman Church. The main issues were the date of Easter and the authority of the Pope. Much bitter debate characterised the Synod but when the discussions were ended and the final decision was taken to adopt the Roman system, Hilda accepted the result without question and the practices at her Whitby monastery were altered accordingly.

Caedmon Cross looks out across Whitby harbour and was unveiled in 1898 by the then Poet Laureate, Alfred Austin. Treasure hunters gain a bonus point for observing the replica Caedmon Cross, made by a member of the school staff, outside Caedmon School.

Abbey Cross stands on steps on Abbey Plain and is a tall octagonal shaft with only a very small part of its crosspiece remaining. Pevsner is uncertain whether it was the medieval market cross of the Abbey Plain or the cross of the abbey burial ground.

Special Interest – WALK 23

Smuggling, we have already noticed, was an important part of the 18th century economy at numerous locations along the North-east Coast but Robin Hood's Bay is regarded as perhaps being the single most important centre. It is hard not to read the accounts of this mammoth tax evasion system without feeling some sense of admiration (and amusement) for the ingenuity and spirit of adventure which smuggling engendered. But it was illegal; dangerous and the participants risked possible deportation or hanging.

All manner of goods were smuggled into the country in order to avoid paying import taxes but the main goods were luxury items such as rum, brandy, gin, wine, tea, coffee, perfumes, silks, lace, tobacco, chocolate and even playing cards. The French Wars against Napoleon meant the Government was constantly needing extra revenue and by 1815 over 1400 different

trade. Squire Farsyde, for example, had a stone slab set in his front lawn at Thorpe Hall to conceal an underground chamber used for storing contraband. We pass Thorpe Hall on Walk 23. Not to have been involved with smuggling would have immediately caused suspicion among the close-knit community.

However, if you were a farmer and unwilling to risk being too closely associated with the traffic, you could nevertheless leave a rested and well-fed horse in a particular stable, with harness and muffling 'boots' at hand, just in case it needed to be 'borrowed' during the night. If the farmer found his horse sweating in the stable the following morning, he could always say it had been hag-ridden by witches. From this superstition, it is said that we get the word 'nightmare'.

The illegality of the smuggling trade must have posed a problem for John Wesley when he came to Robin Hood's Bay. He had spoken out strongly against it in Cornwall but made no reference to the immorality of the communal activity during his numerous visits to Bay Town.

By the end of the 1820s smuggling had become less attractive as import duties were gradually reduced and the coastguard service became more efficient. But it led one person to bemoan the passing of time: 'Alas ... poor folks ha'nt got the means o' bettering themselves like proper Christians'.

St Stephen's (Old) Church, Fylingdales

(942059) lies just off the Cleveland Circles route but is accessible by car along the B1447 road. The church was built in 1821-22 looking out to sea on a site where people have worshipped for many centuries. There is a windswept exterior but a peaceful interior in a building which has been described as a real 'preaching box' with galleries on two sides, box pews below and a three-decker pulpit along the south side. The church contains memorials to shipwrecked sailors as well as 'maiden's garlands' which were carried in the funeral procession of a young girl. **St Stephen's (New) Church**, built in 1870, is located on the edge of Baytown.

Hawsker Cross stands just a few metres from the roadside in Low Hawsker. Pevsner notes the intertwined Viking trails design and thinks there may also be a cockerel and a dragon on the shaft. He suggests it might date from the first half of the 11th century. If the cross is still in its original position, this indicates that there was probably once a church on the site.

commodities were subject to import duties. Ironically, of course, Napoleon welcomed the smuggling trade because it took English cash back to France at the very time when the two countries were at war.

Smuggling lost the British Exchequer huge sums of money: one pound of tea, for example, cost 7d in Holland but sold legally in Britain for 24 shillings. Distilleries in France and Holland produced alcohol specially for the smuggling market.

Robin Hood's Bay was the headquarters of one of the North-east's most powerful smuggling syndicates. Organisation of the traffic was a complex operation. After the contraband had been landed on the beach it had to be distributed as efficiently as possible. It's said that in Robin Hood's Bay there were so many secret passageways between the closely packed houses that it was possible to pass a bale of silk from the shore to the top of the village without it ever appearing above the ground.

Patricia Labistour, in her book 'A Rum Do', tells some amusing tales of the subterfuges used by the smugglers. There were, of course, secret storage places on board the ships. Tea, for example, was hidden under the false floor of one boat's dog kennel. On shore, spirits could be carried around in pigs' bladders and supposedly pregnant women could conceal a surprising volume of goods beneath their voluminous skirts. 'Lingers Ghost' was a local farmer dressed in a white shroud who regularly patrolled the road between Robin Hood's Bay and Fylingthorpe when a smuggling run was due – pity a lonely young Revenue officer, suddenly startled by the moaning apparition on a dark night!

It seems fair to say that majority of the Bay Town population was connected with the smuggling

WALK 23
near HAWSKER – ROBIN HOOD'S BAY

Map: Explorer OL 27
S.E.P.: Lay-by on A171 at Hawsker (925077).
           Toilets at R.H.B. and Fylingthorpe
Buses: 93, 93A
Cleveland Way distance: **3.7 miles**
Circular walk distance: **9.2 miles**
Shorter walk alternative: **6.9 miles**
Special interest:
    Robin Hood's Bay
Cross: Hawsker Cross (923076)

More varied farmland, wooded stream valleys, spectacular cliff scenery and the old smugglers' haunt of Robin Hood's Bay ('Baytown') make this a most enjoyable walk. Free parking is available in the lay-by on the A171 at Hawsker, although it is possible to begin the walk from either of the pay-and-display car parks in Robin Hood's Bay. The shorter walk uses the Rail Trail track to return to Hawsker.

From the lay-by on the A171 we cross the road and retrace the route to the coastline that was used, in reverse direction, on Walk 22. This means walking into High Hawsker and then taking the bridleway on our left next to the bus shelter. The wide track brings us to Gnipe Howe Farm where we go through one gate and are then directed immediately right through another gate, across a field corner and then along the field edge to the cliff path by the memorial seat with its delightful little garden at (1).

Navigation for the next three miles from here to Robin Hood's Bay is simple; views are once again stunning and we cross three N.T. properties each with open access concessions. Where Oakham Beck reaches Maw Wyke Hole is the point (2) at which the Coast to Coast Walk reaches the North Sea before continuing to Robin Hood's Bay.

When we reach the town the short walk doubles back along the disused rail track (3). The long walk carries on down Mount Pleasant North Road to the B1447, turns left along Station Road and then continues down the steep slope to the old centre of 'Baytown'

where there's an opportunity for refreshment as well as much to explore. Treasure hunters do well to turn left at the row of houses named Bloomswell.

The main road, New Road, joins King Street at The Dock, by the Bay Hotel and at the end of the 192-mile Coast to Coast Walk. At this point, if the tide is well out, it is safe to walk along the beach to Stoupe Beck. However, if there is any doubt whatsoever, we have to turn right up Albion Road just before New Road ends. We then take the third set of steps up on our left – the Flagstaff Steps – and, 179 steps later, we reach the top of the cliff. What a wonderful opportunity to slow the party down by pretending to view the magnificent vista

below! Then we continue for a few hundred metres to the path turn turning inland at (4). This takes us round Farsyde House stud farm and then along the tarred Mark Lane to Middlewood Lane (5).

Turning right, we now walk into Fylingthorpe. We cross the ford over King's Beck, go past Thorpe Hall and then turn left at the crossroads by

the Methodist Church. We continue past the toilets to the p.r.o.w. on the right at (6). This has not been clearly indicated when I have walked the route but the turn-off is next to the house called Greystones and the path soon becomes a double-hedged track.

When we come out on the tarred road, we go right for 90m and, immediately after Harton House Farm, go through

the kissing gate on the left (7) and follow the p.r.o.w. up the left-hand side of the field. After another gate we soon cross a stream and turn sharp right up steps and over two stiles before bending right and following the field boundary with the stream below on our right.

At the stone stile (8) we carry on in the same direction up the road through Raw as far as the track on our left at (9). We take this track and a notice board tells us that it leads towards High Normanby. However, care is needed as we approach the first buildings: we go left for 40m and then turn abruptly right to locate the stile and path at the right of the barn. The next section of the route may be overgrown in summer but there are good views of Whitby and another six stiles later we reach the A171 road (10).

The p.r.o.w. does not use the farm drive directly ahead to Fern Farm but instead there is another stile on the left which leads us across a field to a line of old hawthorn trees and from there we continue adjacent to the trees – they are intermittent but clearly show our route. At the two gates (11) we turn right to follow Hawsker Intake Road, at first a grassy greenway and then an earthen track.

When we come to the tarmac (12) we bear right. Then shortly after Mitten Hill Farm we branch left down to the ford and go past the ancient cross back into Low Hawsker.

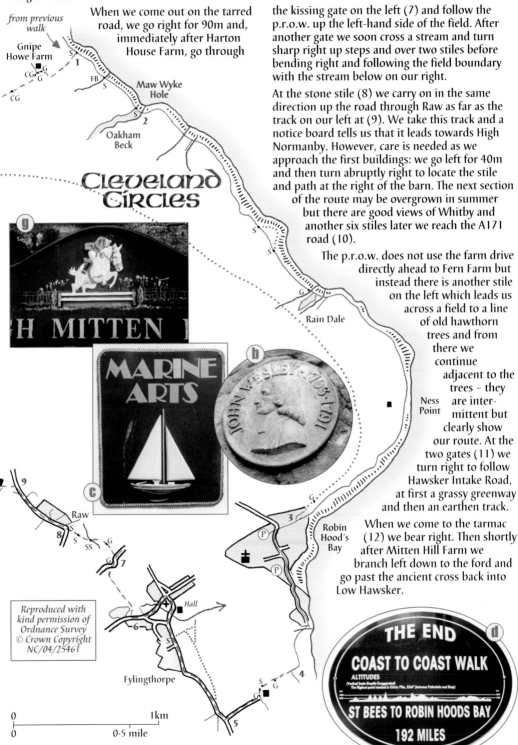

Reproduced with kind permission of Ordnance Survey © Crown Copyright NC/04/25461

WALK 24
ROBIN HOOD'S BAY – RAVENSCAR

Map: Explorer OL 27
S.E.P.T: Ravenscar (980015)
Bus: 16
Cleveland Way distance: **3.1 miles**
Circular walk distance: **10.8 miles**
Shorter walk alternatives:
     East loop   **7.5 miles**
     North-west loop **5.0 miles**
     South loop   **7.7 miles**
Special interest:
     Ravenscar, Ramsdale Mill, Lyke Wake Walk
Cross or Stone: Lyke Wake Walk (971012)

For this walk we start at Ravenscar, walk clockwise and finish the day with the CW section along the cliff top. This enables us to park freely along Raven Hall Road close to the toilets. The shorter walk goes down Raven Hall Road, turns left past the N.T. Visitor Centre, forks left at the Rail Trail indicator and then follows the disused railway back to Robin Hood's Bay. This route can be further split into two by using the road link at Stoupebrow Cottage Farm.

There's a great variety of scenery – grouse moorland, bluebell woods, waterfalls, rolling farmland, glorious displays of gorse as well as the next section of cliff walking. Oh yes; and the familiar stretch of mud, so have appropriate footwear.

Those doing the longer walk go inland up Raven Hall Road and turn right down the green track at Crag Hill house. By the fingerpost at the track crossing (1) we turn left through the gate and go up the hillside to the road at Coney Springs. Turning right, we continue a little way beyond the end of the tarmac to the stile on our left (2). From here the path twists up the hillside to another stile where we join the path on the other side of the wall, turn left and go to the telecommunications pylon (3).

Choosing carefully the broad track to the *right* of the LWW marker stone, we now follow the Lyke Wake Walk over the open heather grouse moor. (The trig point 100m on our left confirms we are on the correct route.) At the waymarked track crossing (4) by the Stony Marl Howes, which we can see on our left, we leave the LWW and bear right following a clear green track through the heather. Then at the track intersection by Cook House (5), we take the bridleway signposted to Robin Hood's Bay.

Going through the farmstead, we continue between fence and wall and then come to a gate where the path bends left and takes us down to a concrete drive (6). Turning right, we follow the waymarks through Spring Hill Farm, then continue on a stony track round to 'Harry's Folly'. Soon the road crosses a small stream and then we come round to Colcroft Farm (7).

The shorter circuit turns right on the road; the longer walk goes left for about 430m to the indicator post half-hidden in the hedge on our right (8). Going through the gate, we continue along the fence for 60m, turn 90° right at the wall, follow the wall down to the beck and continue up the steep slope to the field corner at (9). It may be muddy but we go on

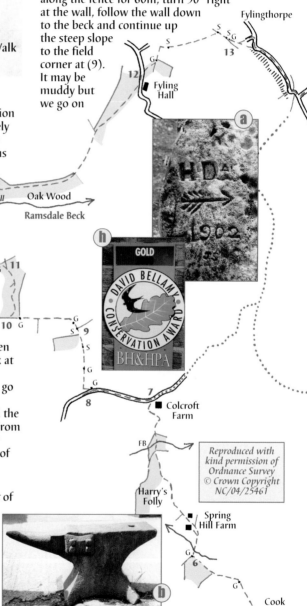

ahead for 70m to the fingerpost and then turn left and follow the wall on our left. We pass through a gate at the edge of the wood and then soon turn back right on ourselves (10). The next few hundred metres may be very muddy in winter but otherwise the woodland is attractive and after we have avoided the right branch at (11) it becomes drier underfoot.

We swing right and walk above the steep side of Kirk Moor Beck before bending down left to Ramsdale Mill. As we approach there's a good view of the mill weir and then a delightful surprise at the mill itself ...

The track carries on at the other side of the beck. After a mile or so when we come to Fyling Hall School we follow the road ahead for about 60m to the indicator post on the right (12). A way-marked path on a renovated trod now takes us round to Sunnyside Farm

and then to The Peat House. Turning right, then soon climbing the stile on our right, we cross a field and follow the hedge in the direction of Fylingthorpe.

We turn right at the stile by the end of the long field and 30m beyond the next stile we go left through the kissing gate by the edge of the houses (13). Bending right, we soon then take the p.r.o.w. along the right-hand side of the houses to join Middlewood Lane. From here we bear right and re-trace the route used on Walk 23 going along Middlewood Lane as far as Mark Lane and there turning left to reach the CW at the coast (14).

From now on it's easy navigation all the way to Ravenscar. However we should be prepared for the steep descents and ascents at Boggle Hole and Stoupe Beck. If we're lucky we may hear the peacocks at Stoupebrow Cottage Farm (15) from where the short circuit link road leads to the disused railway.

When we reach the fingerpost at (16) we should certainly not miss the chance of making a short detour left to look at the remains of the Peak Alum Works. Returning to the CW we follow the indicators for another mile or so back up the quarry face and into Ravenscar.

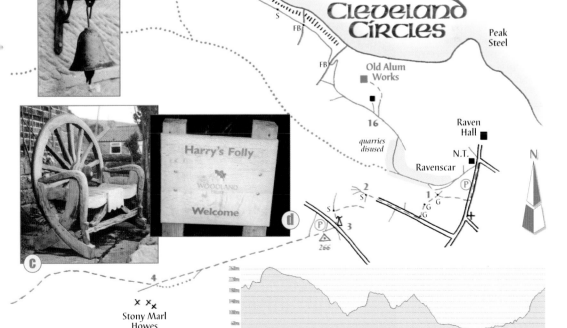

Special Interest – WALK 24

Water Mills and Windmills Cleveland Circles Walks have already passed a number of water and windmill sites and it may be useful at this stage to review the different types of mills found in North-east Yorkshire. John Harrison's account in the 'Historical Atlas of North Yorkshire' suggests that mill sites in the region can be roughly arranged into the following groups according to their type and age.

(a) Most corn mill sites are **medieval** in origin and therefore often older than generally assumed. Almost every village had its own water mill and feudal custom dictated that all grain should be ground at the 'lord's mill' where the lord would take a share of the grain. Good relics of these early mills survive at Caydale and Arden. However, some larger townships like Helmsley, Guisborough and Great Ayton had two mills on separate sites. Even in some moorland dales the spread of ploughing allowed the development of secondary 'nether mills' or 'low mills' as in Bilsdale. Monasteries often had their own mills.

(b) Mills operated by **windpower** rather than by water became common in the 13th and 14th centuries especially along the Tees estuary but also along the coast and in Ryedale but the sites of these 'post' windmills are often not known because their wooden structures have disappeared. Post mills are mills pivoted on a post.

(c) References to **'double mills'** (mills with two water wheels each driving its own set of millstones) are found in 16th and 17th century records and these bigger watermills were located at prosperous settlements around the moorland margins at places like Hinderwell and Osmotherley.

(d) Industrialisation and urbanisation in the 18th and 19th centuries meant that older mills could not cope with the increased demands for wheat flour. Large numbers of older mills were therefore rebuilt and these **'improved mills'**, with their additional storeys on top, could provide extra space for storage and machinery. Good working examples are found at Low Mill in Bilsdale as well as the fine restored mill at Tocketts. In addition new large watermills were constructed by the coast, e.g. on Mill Beck (Boggle Hole) near Robin Hood's Bay and along the lower Esk River at Ruswarp. Scalby Beck had four mills along its lower waterside.

(e) The Industrial Revolution period also saw the development of large, brick-built **tower windmills** that were specially equipped with French burr millstones for producing high quality flour. Relatively few of these survive in the region but examples can be seen at Hawsker, Ravenscar, Whitby and Scarborough. 'Tower' mills (or smock mills) are windmills with a fixed tower and a revolvable cap above bearing the sails.

(f) North-east Yorkshire also possesses a fine heritage of **estate water mills** dating from about 1790-1855. These include converted or maintained buildings at Easby, Ingleby Greenhow, Raisdale, Rievaulx, Oldstead and Kepwick.

Boggle Hole is one of several former mills that have been saved from dereliction by being converted into Youth Hostels but the spectacular restoration and new wheel at **Ramsdale Mill** is in a class of its own. It is believed that there has been a water-wheel on the site since the 11th century and that mill may have been the 'Fieling mill' granted, along with several other mills, in 1102 by William de Percy to Whitby Abbey. A new mill had to be built in 1858 after a disastrous flood in the previous year but the present superb wheel is the creation of Peter McQue and was only commissioned in 2003. The aim eventually is to create hydro-electric power at the site.

The Bay reveals a magnificent wave-cut platform when the tide is out. The great sweeping crescent shaped reefs ('scars' as known locally) are the remains of a huge dome structure centred on the Bay. As the sea has gradually eaten into the structure, the different layers of rock have been revealed.

The Lyke Wake Walk Stone marks one end of the classic walk between Osmotherley and Ravenscar pioneered in 1955 by Bill Cowley. In order to try to reduce pressure on this route, two alternative challenges, the Lyke Wake Way (50 miles) and the Shepherds' Round (40 miles) have been devised.

Special Interest – WALK 25

Ravenscar When the Peak Estate Company purchased Peak Hall and the surrounding land in the 1890s, there were plans for turning it into 'the most bracing health resort on the east coast'. Land was cleared and plots were put up for sale. To avoid confusion with the Peak District in Derbyshire, the Peak Company was renamed the Ravenscar Estate Company and Peak Hall changed its name to Raven Hall. The plans never came to fruition and the Company was declared bankrupt in 1913. Excellent displays at the N.T. Centre give details of the failed venture as well as information about the alum-making process. The Centre is open from May to October.

Green Dike is thought to be the former southern boundary of St.Hilda's Whitby Abbey land.

Three Lords' Stones need careful punctuation. They are the stones of three lords; not three stones.

WALK 25
RAVENSCAR –
HAYBURN WYKE

Map: Explorer OL 27
S.E.P.T.: Ravenscar (980015)
Bus: 16
Cleveland Way distance: **4.3 miles**
Circular walk distance: **11.0 miles**
Shorter walk alternatives:
    North loop   **7.9 miles**
    South loop   **6.7 miles**
Special interest:
    Hayburn Wyke, Ravenscar
Cross or Stone: Three Lords' Stones (969002)

Once more there's a variety of scenery on this walk: CW coastal cliffs, woodland tracks, heather moors and undulating farmland. The bridleway between War Dike Lane and Island Farm allows the creation of two medium distance loops. Alternatively by using the War Dike link and the disused rail track it is possible to create two short walks, although it will be necessary to request permission for parking at the Hayburn Wyke Hotel for the southern loop.

The full circuit starts and finishes at the same point as Walk 24 by the toilets on Raven Hall Road, Ravenscar, but this time we complete the CW section first.

Walking down Raven Hall Road, we turn right on Station Road, then left at the CW indicator to Scarborough. At the cliff edge (1) we turn right and make our way to Hayburn. This remote stretch of the coast was notorious for smuggling and the O.S. map shows a p.r.o.w. running through the undulations of the fallen cliff material below us; perhaps it was just as inaccessible 250 years ago as it appears today. On the way we observe the Rocket Post and the former Bent Rigg coastguard

lookout post before we reach the path to War Dike Lane (2). This is the turn-off point for either of the two northern loops.

Unlike the last walk there's only one significant stream cutting across this section of the CW – that's Hayburn Beck which we reach down steep steps. It's a glorious spot to pause before we have to climb the steps on the other side of the valley. Following the acorn and ignoring minor turn-offs, we keep to the main path

up through the damp woodland. Then at the fingerpost (3) before we come to the top of the valley, we leave the CW going left and instead bear right to a waymarked stile at the edge of the N.T. property. Crossing a small field and bending right at the gate, we come to the Hayburn Wyke Hotel.

We take the tarred p.r.o.w. that goes back left and then swings right to the disused railway where we turn right and follow the track to the bridge overhead (4). Here we scramble up the far right side in order to reach the path at the top. We turn right across the bridge to a stile and then continue to the minor road (5). Going right again, we walk past Hayburn Beck Farm to the road bend at (6) and here take the track on the left towards Cloughton Moor.

The cobbled track going up to and through the trees leads to a pleasant change of scenery and, following the red arrows, we continue to Cloughton Moor House. From here we stay on the red-arrowed route going N.W. along the right-hand edge of the forest but we should be prepared for this being very muddy in wet weather.

Crossing the stream and stile at Prior Wath (7) we then go up over a field to pass through the gate in the opposite corner. We follow the edge of the trees and bend right at the wall. At the road corner (8) we go left, then left again down the track to Island Farm.

The bridleway turns right in front of the farm and we go through two gates. Then we follow the hedge and field boundary to the thick hedge facing us at (9). Turning left we go down to cross Thorny Beck and then continue up to the sideroad adjacent to the A171. The legal p.r.o.w. goes left for 70m parallel with the road and then we double back on ourselves and walk along the sideroad to the Falcon Inn.

Our route turns right immediately before we reach the pub – the fingerpost directs us through the garden area – and then we cross a small field behind the pub to a waymarked stile.

We continue along the path at the side of the forest and then after about 300m we join the

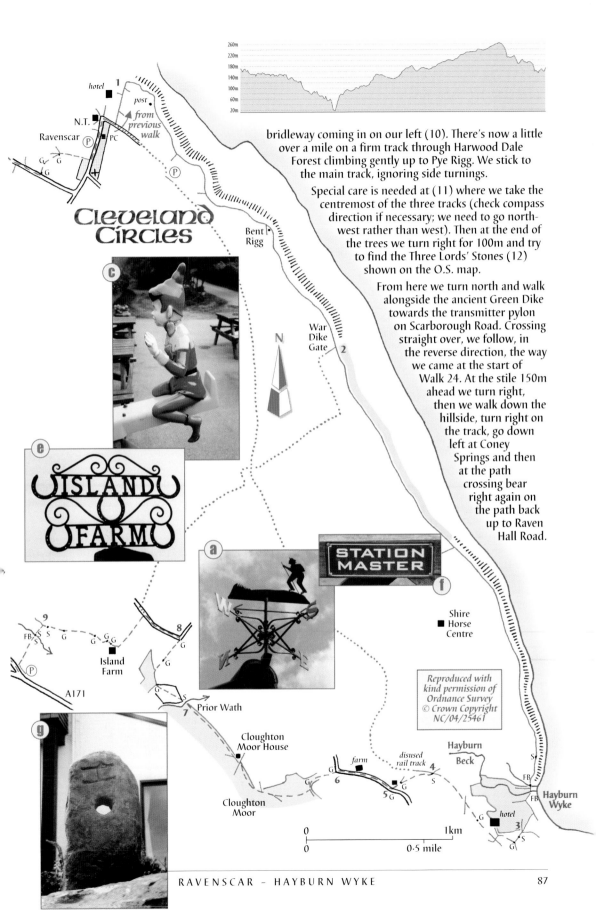

Cleveland Circles

hotel **1**

post

from previous walk

N.T.

Ravenscar P PC

G G
G

Bent Rigg

War Dike Gate **2**

N

bridleway coming in on our left (10). There's now a little over a mile on a firm track through Harwood Dale Forest climbing gently up to Pye Rigg. We stick to the main track, ignoring side turnings.

Special care is needed at (11) where we take the centremost of the three tracks (check compass direction if necessary; we need to go north-west rather than west). Then at the end of the trees we turn right for 100m and try to find the Three Lords' Stones (12) shown on the O.S. map.

From here we turn north and walk alongside the ancient Green Dike towards the transmitter pylon on Scarborough Road. Crossing straight over, we follow, in the reverse direction, the way we came at the start of Walk 24. At the stile 150m ahead we turn right, then we walk down the hillside, turn right on the track, go down left at Coney Springs and then at the path crossing bear right again on the path back up to Raven Hall Road.

STATION MASTER

Shire Horse Centre

Reproduced with kind permission of Ordnance Survey © Crown Copyright NC/04/25461

9
FB S S G
S G G G
P **8** G
Island Farm G

A171

7 Prior Wath

Cloughton Moor House

farm

disused rail track **4**

Hayburn Beck

Hayburn Wyke

FB
FB

hotel **3**
S
G

6 G G
5 G

Cloughton Moor

0 ——————— 1km
0 ——————— 0·5 mile

WALK 26
HAYBURN WYKE – CROOK NESS

Map: Explorer OL 27
S.E.P.:   Crook Ness (026936)
Buses to Burniston: 93, 93A, 15, 16
Cleveland Way distance: **3.1 miles**
Circular walk distance: **12.0 miles**
Shorter walk alternative: **6.8 miles**
Special interest:
    Standingstones Rigg Stone Circle
Cross or Stone:
    Standingstones Rigg Stone Circle (983970)

There's more fine cliff scenery on this walk as well as the opportunity to visit the prehistoric stone circle at Standingstones Rigg. Unofficial parking is possible at Cloughton Wyke or by the disused railway track but the route description assumes that we begin at the designated parking area at Crook Ness. As on Walk 25 the use of the disused rail track permits a shorter itinerary to be completed.

From Crook Ness we take the road to Cliff Top House, turn left along Field Lane and walk to the disused railway (1). We climb up to the rail track (steps are on the far left side of the bridge) and follow this to Station Lane, Cloughton (2). Here the shorter walk continues straight on while the longer walk turns left down Station Lane.

Station Lane brings us to the main A171 and, going straight across, we take the path leading over Cloughton Beck to the bottom of Quarry Banks. Going through a stile we turn left on a well-used track round the edge of the overgrown quarries. Ignoring side-paths, we reach the road corner (3) and bear right on the tarmac which soon becomes a dirt path. We continue along the edge of a field before the path divides and, avoiding the left branch going down the slope, we bend right. Two fields later we come to Ripley's Road (4).

Crossing straight over, we keep the wall on our left as we go alongside two fields to Cloughton Woods. Now we either take the path, through the gorse, in the left field corner or use the gate slightly to our right to reach the path that bends down left and joins the first path. From this point we carry on down to the footbridge over Oxdale Slack and then up to the fingerpost at the path T-junction (5). Turning left, we are led round to Gowland Lane. We go right-left on the tarmac and

then follow the waymarks round field edges to Harwood Dale Road (6).

Turning right again we follow the road for a little over half a mile to the track on our right (7) just after the road to Thirley Cote Farm. We now follow the edge of the F.C. plantation to the corner of the forest at (8). Here we bend round to the left and, ignoring the first cross-track, walk for a total of 660m to the second crossing. Now we turn right and continue on the stony forest drive to where the plantation on our right comes to an end (9).

Clevelan∂ Circles

Another right turn leads us on a muddy path beside the wall until we come to the standing stones on our left – this is a Cleveland Circle par excellence! A little further along the wall we have permission to use the small gate to cross to Standing Stones Rigg Farm and from the farmhouse we continue to the main A171 road. Please remember that this concessionary access is a goodwill gesture from the farmer and in no way indicates any general right of public access. Turning right on the A171 we walk with great care on the grass verge to the fingerpost on our left (10).

The path through the trees is reasonably clear, though we mustn't miss the waymark directing us right down the slope, and as we keep going down yellow marker blobs give some help in bringing us to Cloughton Moor House. From here we turn right and for a few hundred metres follow, in

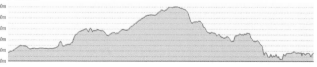

reverse, the same route that we used on Walk 25.

We go as far as the fingerpost pointing us to Cloughton (11) and here we turn right. We ignore a p.r.o.w. going off right but when we reach a recently cleared and replanted area (it was like this in 2005) we need to bear left (12) in order to stay on route. Going down to cross a rather boggy patch, we are then led up alongside a wall to the road at (13). A left turn down the hill brings us to the pillar box where we go right and once again pick up the route of Walk 25. We follow the path to the disused rail track, turn right towards the Hayburn Wyke Hotel, leave the rail track to reach the hotel on our left and from there bend right to the stile at the edge of the N.T. property (14).

Just inside the N.T. area we rejoin the C.W. but this time we turn right and carry on up the steps to the edge of the woodland. From here there's about three miles of easy cliff walking to Crook Ness. The blackthorn hedges are a particular attraction in spring. On the way we see the former coastguard lookout hut, now a bird-watching hide, on Long Nab.

Crook Ness ravine, we learn from the information board, has always provided good access to the shore and used to provide access for pannier-laden donkeys carrying road-building stone. The track was blown up in World War II to prevent enemy access but has since been rebuilt.

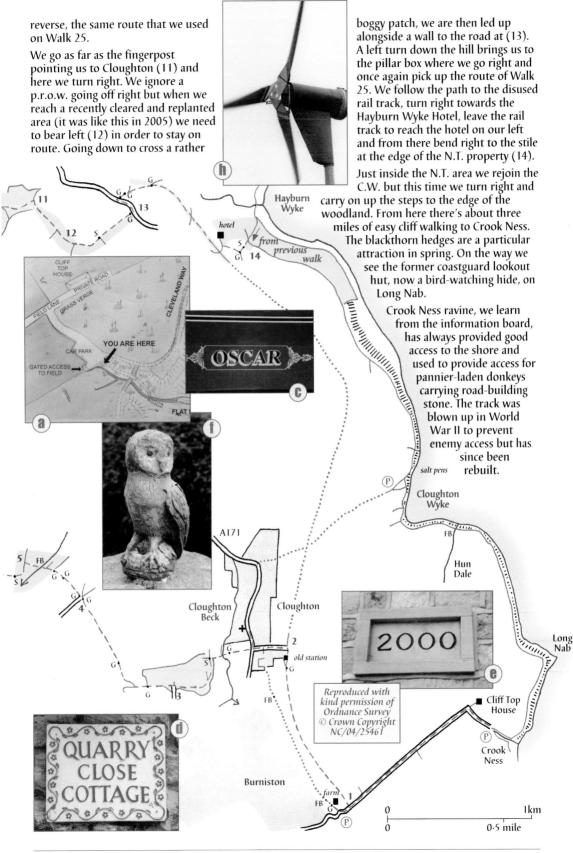

Special Interest – WALK 26

Standingstones Rigg Small Stone Circle lies on the property of Anne Tiffany and I am very grateful for her kindness in allowing Cleveland Circles walkers to cross her farmland in order to view this ancient monument.

The ring of stones on Standingstones Rigg is classed by archaeologists as a 'small stone circle'. This can be defined as a ring of between 7 and 16 stones with a diameter of between 4 and 20 metres. Of the 250 or so stone circles identified in England over 100 are classed as the 'small' variety.

Where excavated, stone circles have been found to date from the Late Neolithic to the Middle Bronze Age (about 2400 - 1000 BC). Archaeologists agree that these monuments had considerable ritual importance for the societies that used them. In many cases, such as at Standingstones Rigg, they provided a focus for burial rituals. Other circles, like those at Stonehenge and Avebury, appear to have had a calendrical function with the stones being carefully aligned to mark important solar or lunar events such as sunrise or sunset at midsummer or midwinter.

The small circle at Standingstones Rigg comprises a ring of 15 earthfast stones, although originally there were 24 in the circle, some having been removed over time. Two small hollows within the ring are the result of past excavation which un- covered a burial site that included stones etched with cup and ring marks. 'Cup and ring marks' have been described as a type of prehistoric rock art. These decorations are found in many parts of upland Britain on both natural rock outcrops and on portable stones placed next to burial sites. Small hollows are pecked into the rock surface and these 'cups' may be surrounded by one or more 'rings'. About 800 examples of prehistoric rock art have been recorded in England.

Special Interest – WALK 27

Scalby Parish Church is dedicated to St Laurence and a visit is highly recommended. There was a church in Scalby at least as early as 1130 because documents from Bridlington Priory record the gift by Eustace Fitzjohn of a church in Scalby to the Priory of Bridlington. The Norman chancel arch and the nave arcade arches date from about 1180.

As we enter the building we are reminded of the Christian injunction 'Pra Remember the Power' ('Pray Remember the Poor') and below the notice is a carved oak Jacobean poor box. The pulpit and Communion Table are also Jacobean.

In the modern (1960) east window we see the story of St Laurence who, as a deacon under the Bishop of Rome in 258, had the care of the church's valuables of money, vessels and vestments. When he was ordered by the secular authority to account for these treasures, Laurence refused. Instead, he is said to have gathered the sick, the poor and the children to whom he had ministered and declared: 'Behold here are the treasures of Christ's Church'. For this he was led away and, according to the tradition shown in the window, was tortured to death, stretched on a gridiron. Modern scholars believe that, like his Bishop and other contemporary martyrs, he was beheaded.

Perhaps Scalby's most famous vicar was William Mompesson. Although he was in Scalby for less than a year, his later story is one of extraordinary courage and sacrifice. William Mompesson became vicar of Eyam in Derbyshire. In 1665 the plague came to Eyam and William, helped by Thomas Stanley, the previous rector, declared Eyam to be in voluntary quarantine so that villagers would not spread the disease to surrounding areas. Of the 350 people who had not escaped from Eyam, only 83 survived.

One of the church's special possessions is its sundial, donated in 1690, which stands outside the porch. The churchyard is also home to the coralroot bittercress plant, a purple flower that grows here in abundance but is not known elsewhere in the district. The guide booklet relates the story of the vicar who, after baptising Mabel Trott in 1714 wrote in the Church Register 'a ridiculous name given her because she was born on Mayday'. One did not, of course, have to worry about political correctness in those days.

Water Mills There used to be four water-powered corn mills sited alongside the lower stretch of Scalby Beck. The **Old Scalby Mills** pub, formerly known as Scalby Low Mill, was one of these. It was often damaged by flooding and choked by 'the immense quantity of debris including trees, broken bridges and dead pigs' that the floodwaters brought downstream. By 1850 the main building had become a hotel. The mill by the bridge on Whitby Road became a Youth Hostel.

Cross: Millennium Commemoration Cross (AD 2000) erected by Scalby Village Trust.

To visit **The Dinosaur Beach** is a wonderful experience but access can be a little tricky. I was privileged to spend a fascinating couple of hours with Will Watts investigating the dinosaur prints at the Jackson Bay Dinosaur Trackway and a little further north at Sailors' Grave; I confess I was hooked! Dinosaur footprints were first identified on the Yorkshire coast as long ago as 1895 and most of the prints are of three-toed (tridactyl) creatures though there are a few five-toed (pentadactyl) remains. Size varies from 3 cm to over 50 cm. In all, over 20 different types of animal have been identified but there are two basic kinds of remains we can spot. Some, like those in the Trackway, appear as

Jackson Bay Dinosaur Trackway. Cobbles indicate the position of three-toed footprints

hollows in the surface rock. Most, however, stand slightly raised above the level of the surrounding rock. It is thought that in these cases the prints were first made in soft silt or fine sand and then harder material was washed into the print hollows. This material was better able to resist erosion and therefore remained proud when the softer rock around it was later worn away.

Cliff falls expose fresh dinosaur prints

Sadly, the Dinosaur footprints have been subjected to vandalism as collectors have broken off and taken away specimen fossils. It seems staggering that prehistoric remains that have lasted for some 160 million years should be stolen and carried off overnight. The National Park has to perform a very difficult balancing act as, on the one hand, it tries to protect what are truly national treasures of unique import-ance and on the other hand, it tries to encourage widespread public appreciation of our coastal heritage. For this reason, it is recommended that would-be footprint hunters first contact the Dinosaur Coast Project Manager (01723 383636) or visit the website www.dinocoast.org.uk .

WALK 27
CROOK NESS –
SCALBY MILLS

Map: Explorer OL 27
S.E.P.: Crook Ness (026936)
Buses to Burniston: 93, 93A, 15, 16
Cleveland Way distance: **2.3 miles**
Circular walk distance: **9.4 miles**
Shorter walk alternative: **6.4 miles**
Special interest:
   Crook Ness, Sea Cut-Scalby Beck, Scalby
   village & St Laurence Church, Dinosaur
   Beach
Cross: Millennium Commemoration Cross
   AD 2000 (020904)

This walk has the standard mix of sea cliffs, wooded tracks, moorland edge, farmland and picturesque village. But the sea monsters at the Oceanarium can be left until the next walk. Those preferring a shorter route have the option of using the disused rail track ('Trailway') as on the last two walks.

If we start from the official car park at Crook Ness this means we begin the CW coastal section immediately. However, parking is also permitted along Scalby Mills Road and this would mean we would finish the itinerary with the cliff walk. It is also possible for a few cars to park adjacent to the Trailway on the edge of Burniston and so complete the road section down Field Lane at the very beginning of the walk.

Setting off from Crook Ness we take the tarmac path leading towards the sea, go up the steps on our right and then follow the cliff edge to Scalby Mills. If the tide is out, the wave-cut platform is quite spectacular and we have the chance to dream about Jurassic Park because the section of rocky shore from Sailors' Grave southwards contains some of the finest dinosaur footprints in the country. Less romantic, just before we reach Scalby Mills, is the sight of the sewer pipe at Scalby Ness Sands.

Scalby Beck carries the waters of the Sea Cut which helps to drain the Vale of Pickering and after we have descended the steps to cross the footbridge over the beck, we turn immediately right at the Old Scalby Mills pub and walk up the road (1).

We continue along Scalby Mills Road to the A165, turn right, cross over and then take the first road on our left, Hillcrest Avenue. At the end of the houses the path goes on for 60m and then forks. The branch bending right is preferable but it later curves round to join the left fork at (2). We then continue, with the houses on our right, on a gritty path to join a tarred section of the Trailway a short distance ahead.

Turning right, we are led across two suburban roads and over Scalby Beck before we wiggle through the houses and come to Station Road. Here the short circuit uses Field Close Road, ahead and slightly to the right, before rejoining the Trailway. The longer walk turns left, crosses Scalby Road (A171) and continues straight ahead down High Street into Scalby village.

We bear left at the Methodist Church hall and then should not miss the opportunity to visit the Parish Church of St Laurence on our right. A very informative guide booklet is available.

Leaving the churchyard on the south side and turning right, there's a fine spot on the green for a picnic before we follow the tarmac p.r.o.w. called Carr Lane (3). This soon becomes an earth track, possibly muddy, and leads for about half a mile along the edge of attractive woodland

and then for another half mile between hedges to Prospect House Farm (4).

The p.r.o.w. turns right and passes in front of the farm and after 200m bears slightly left across a field. We aim for the gate in the far corner and then walk along the foot of the steep banking on our left. At the end of the pasture we turn sharp right and after three gates reach Limestone Road (5).

Here we bend right along the road, pass Cumboots Farm, cross over the road junction and

then reach the indicator post on the right at (6). The p.r.o.w. here goes over arable land to the stile at the other side of the field. Then going straight over the road, the path continues, with several right-angle turns, round the edge of fields to the T-junction at (7). (The sequence of turns is right, left, left at Washy Cote Beck, right through the hedge and then along the left edge of a long field.) At (7) we turn right, then left through the kissing gate, to arrive opposite The Three Jolly Sailors on the A171 in Burniston.

Going left for 40m, we then turn down Rocks Lane on our right. The road twists a little as we pass Pricky Beck Green Community Wildlife Site and go under the Trailway. Then there's less than a mile back to Crook Ness.

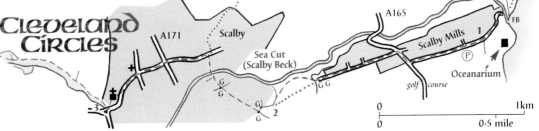

WALK 28
A DAY AT THE SEASIDE

MIND YOUR BUSINESS

Spice Traders
Bar & Wok Restaurant

A New Eating Experience

Open 7 days a week 11am to 11pm

47 **CHEAPEST SHOP IN TOWN** 47

DIGITAL WATCHES FROM £1-00

R.T. Aalten 588 km

INNER WHEEL

HERE LIE THE REMAINS OF
ANNE BRONTË,
DAUGHTER OF THE
REVD. P. BRONTË,
Incumbent of Haworth, Yorkshire.
She died Aged 28
MAY 28TH 1849.

i

n

l

p

j

EST. 1932
A.CASTLE
AND
SONS

STONEMASONS
CARPENTERS
AND
GRAVEDIGGERS

PER·PERICULA· ·IRE·JUVAT·
AD·DECUS

k

o

m

THE THREE MARINERS
THE ANCIENT &
HISTORIC INN
(BUILT 1360)
NOW USED AS A ᴄᴀꜰᴇ HOUSE
THE FAMOUS HAUNT
OF SMUGGLERS
WITH ITS SECRET
HIDING PLACES
PANELLED THROUGHOUT

SCALBY MILLS - HOLBECK

95

WALK 28
SCALBY MILLS – HOLBECK

Map: Explorer 301
S.E.P.: Holbeck car park (049868). Toilets in Scarborough
Buses: 120, 121
Rail to Scarborough
Cleveland Way distance: **3.9 miles**
Circular walk distance: **8.5 miles**
Shorter walk alternatives:
    North loop **4.7 miles**
    South loop **4.5 miles**
Special interest:
    Scarborough Heritage Trail, Scarborough Castle, Gristhorpe Man, Holbeck Hall Hotel
Crosses: St Mary's Church Millennium Cross (047891) or Butter Cross (047888)

There is no designated CW route through the town from Scalby Mills to Holbeck so we are at liberty to devise our own walk. I found the circuit suggested here both varied and interesting though we need to check tide times to determine whether or not we can walk on the two beaches. Anyone wanting to split the walk into two sections could use separate South Bay and North Bay walks.

Starting from the free car park by the former Holbeck Hall Hotel, we walk inland up Sea Cliff Road, turn first right on Holbeck Hill road and then after 90m go right on the tarred footpath into the trees (1). This path saves some road-walking and, avoiding side-paths, comes out on Esplanade Crescent at the Holbeck Clock Tower.

From here we follow the Esplanade to where it bends into Belmont Road (2). We don't turn but carry straight on ahead using the tarred path that takes us over the Spa Footbridge. Then we go left down the steps of Museum Terrace to make an out-and-back detour and visit the unmistakeable Rotunda Museum, which at the time of writing is undergoing major refurbishment. On returning up the steps we turn back left along Cliff Bridge Terrace, take the footbridge over Vernon Road into the park and, soon bearing right, continue past the Yorkshire Coast Homes and on to The Crescent. Turning left we walk to the second exit on our left and this takes us to the roundabout at (3).

From here the suggested route through the town is as follows:

Bear right into Falconer's Road (the fingerpost directs us to the Town Hall) and walk as far as St Nicholas Street. Bend left into St Nicholas Street; go right at the crossroads down Newborough; continue along Eastborough; turn left up the cobbles of West Sandgate; carry on up St Mary's Street and Church Stairs Street to St Mary's Parish Church (4).

St Mary's Church is open during the summer months from Monday to Friday and Anne Bronte's grave in the cemetery on the opposite side of Church Lane is easy to find – it's the one with the floral decorations.

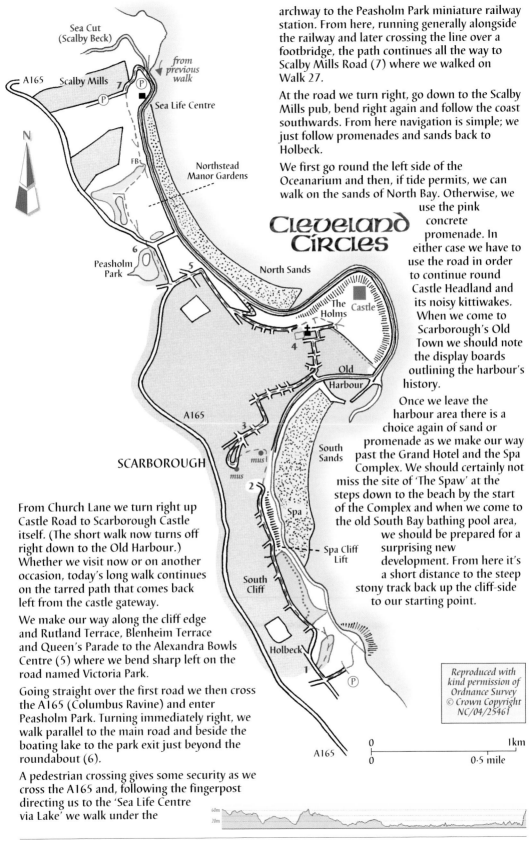

archway to the Peasholm Park miniature railway station. From here, running generally alongside the railway and later crossing the line over a footbridge, the path continues all the way to Scalby Mills Road (7) where we walked on Walk 27.

At the road we turn right, go down to the Scalby Mills pub, bend right again and follow the coast southwards. From here navigation is simple; we just follow promenades and sands back to Holbeck.

We first go round the left side of the Oceanarium and then, if tide permits, we can walk on the sands of North Bay. Otherwise, we use the pink concrete promenade. In either case we have to use the road in order to continue round Castle Headland and its noisy kittiwakes. When we come to Scarborough's Old Town we should note the display boards outlining the harbour's history.

Once we leave the harbour area there is a choice again of sand or promenade as we make our way past the Grand Hotel and the Spa Complex. We should certainly not miss the site of 'The Spaw' at the steps down to the beach by the start of the Complex and when we come to the old South Bay bathing pool area, we should be prepared for a surprising new development. From here it's a short distance to the steep stony track back up the cliff-side to our starting point.

From Church Lane we turn right up Castle Road to Scarborough Castle itself. (The short walk now turns off right down to the Old Harbour.) Whether we visit now or on another occasion, today's long walk continues on the tarred path that comes back left from the castle gateway.

We make our way along the cliff edge and Rutland Terrace, Blenheim Terrace and Queen's Parade to the Alexandra Bowls Centre (5) where we bend sharp left on the road named Victoria Park.

Going straight over the first road we then cross the A165 (Columbus Ravine) and enter Peasholm Park. Turning immediately right, we walk parallel to the main road and beside the boating lake to the park exit just beyond the roundabout (6).

A pedestrian crossing gives some security as we cross the A165 and, following the fingerpost directing us to the 'Sea Life Centre via Lake' we walk under the

Special Interest – WALK 28

Scarborough Castle claims never to have been taken by force - only by starvation or sickness. Castle Mound's commanding position jutting out into the North Sea meant that the only realistic line of attack would have been across the narrow neck of land separating North Bay from South Bay. Its strategic importance was recognised by Bronze Age and Iron Age peoples, both of whom had settlements here. Then about A.D. 370 the Romans built one of their coastal signal stations, a square tower in the middle of a square courtyard and surrounded by a protective ditch. However, the archaeology is complex; the Roman remnants are intermingled with the remains of three different medieval chapels.

It is therefore surprising that when the Vikings came to Scarborough they were satisfied to occupy the land below the cliff and, later on, we might have expected the Normans to have quickly constructed a castle on the hilltop site. However there is no mention of a castle in the Domesday Book and the first Norman work dates from c.1135. This was when William le Gros started the building process, although it was Henry II who was responsible for the construction of the fortress that we see crowning the headland today. To protect the castle from possible landward attack, an extremely impressive curtain wall was built above a deep ditch. A powerful square keep

with corner turrets was erected (1157-1169) behind the wall. Later the defence was further strengthened with a gate and barbican (1174-5).

Its dramatic position on the cliff-top headland has provided the castle with excellent seaward defences but paradoxically there has always been a problem of erosion of the cliffs by the sea. Undercutting at the base of the cliffs caused the undermining of a part of the curtain wall even before 1278 and subsequent attacks by the sea have caused most of the curtain wall at the eastern end of the site to fall away over the cliff. Scarborough Castle witnessed sieges on several occasions but it was during the Civil War that it experienced its greatest tests. The castle was in Royalist hands during the siege of 1645 when the Parliamentarians placed their biggest gun inside the chancel of St Mary's Church in order to try to pound the castle into submission. Such was the

Dan Savage

CLEVELAND CIRCLES

damage done to the keep and the gatehouse that when the starving garrison eventually surrendered they could not come out through the gate but had to exit through the rubble using a hole in the wall. Towards the end of their ordeal, the Royalists had eaten cats, dogs, sparrows and even rats; they had boiled and chewed their leather belts and only 20 of the 200 men left were not wounded. Later, in 1648, the castle was again held for the king and, once more, the garrison was forced to surrender due to starvation. Parliament ordered the castle to be slighted but the military had already inflicted enough damage to make this unnecessary.

Since then Scarborough Castle has not been used except as a prison or a barracks. George Fox, the Quaker dissident, was incarcerated here in 1665 and forced to exist on starvation rations. The last military action seen at the castle was when Scarborough, like Whitby Abbey, was shelled by German warships in 1914. The castle itself was hit and in the town 19 people were killed.

Gristhorpe Man dates from the Middle Bronze Age (about 1600-1400 BC). In 1834 William Beswick supervised the excavations of a prehistoric barrow at Gristhorpe and revealed one of the best preserved burial remains found in North-east Yorkshire. The grave site contained a large hollowed-out oak log. Inside lay a man's skeleton and various very well preserved grave

goods. The tall mature male had been buried wearing an animal skin cloak held in place with a bone pin. The man's bones were immediately removed to a local doctor's surgery where they simmered in a gelatine solution in a copper boiler and were then left to dry. No other conservation treatment has been given to the skeleton. The bones are stained black from iron deposits in the clay combined with tannic acid from the oak coffin. Personal grave objects and the fact of a coffin burial suggest that this was a person of important social standing. Gristhorpe Man resides at the Rotunda Museum.

The **Butter Cross** is the sole survivor of several medieval market crosses in Scarborough. It has been removed from its original site.

St Mary's Church Millennium Cross stands in the grounds of a church which is, we are reminded, 'as old as the castle but in much better condition' – and that is despite the damage inflicted on the building during the Civil War. The Cross is a modern interpretation of a Viking commemorative stone that was erected to mark the Scarborough Viking Festival held in June 2000. It is a reminder of Scarborough's Viking heritage from the end of the first millennium and the conversion of the Viking people to Christianity in 996 AD.

WALK 29
HOLBECK – GRISTHORPE CLIFF

Map: Explorer 301
S.E.P.: Holbeck car park (049868)
Buses: 120, 121
Rail to Scarborough
Cleveland Way distance: **4.2 miles**
Circular walk distance: **11.2 miles**
Shorter walk alternatives:
North loop **4.4 miles**
South loop **7.0 miles**
(from Cayton Bay car park)
Special interest:
Holbeck Hall Hotel, Cayton Sands
Cross or Stone:
Holbeck Hall Hotel memorial stone

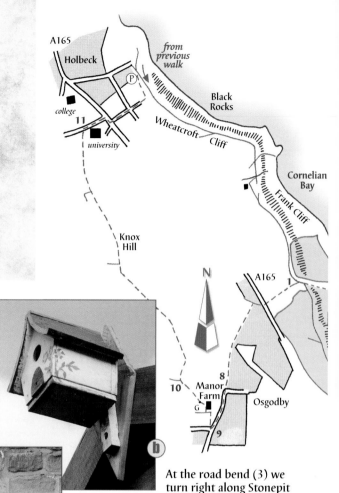

This walk forms a kind of elongated egg-timer with small circuits at either end and a thin central linking section. Parking (with toilets) is available at Cayton Bay Holiday Village but the route description begins at the free car park at Holbeck. Cayton Sands should preferably be walked at low tide. Readers of 'Exploring Lake Pickering' should recognise parts of the present walk.

From Holbeck we follow the CW on the cliff-top path towards Cayton. We pass the golf course on Wheatcroft Cliff (noting the old ridge and furrow field pattern underneath the green sward of the golf turf) and then the pumping station on our right. At the bungalows (1) the short north circuit goes right but the CW and the long walk turn left towards the sea.

We continue on the CW through the wooded N.T. properties of Cayton Cliff and Tenants' Cliff, following the acorns and ignoring side-tracks. The path then becomes more open as we carry on round Cayton Bay to Lebberston Cliff. Staying on the cliff top above Gristhorpe Sands, we reach the fingerpost at (2) directing us right and through the Blue Dolphin Holiday Park towards Gristhorpe.

At the road bend (3) we turn right along Stonepit Lane and right again (4) on the tarred drive to Mount Pleasant Farm. From there we continue to the coastal path (5) where we walked earlier in the day. Now we go left and retrace our steps as far as the path leading up left to the car park (6). At this point, we turn right and go down to Cayton Sands. There is now an enjoyable stride along the beach to the northern end of the Bay.

Near the end of the sands there is an old World War II pill-box. We ignore the set of steps going up the cliff 100m before this lookout and instead carry on for about 100m after the pill-box to a small pond trapped at the foot of the cliff. From here two paths lead up the slope; we take the less obvious one to the right of the pool (7) and this brings us back up to the Cleveland Way. We need to turn right for a short

distance to reach the path junction at the corner of the bungalows (1) where we now go left in order to complete the long walk's northern loop.

Crossing the A165, we go up Reservoir Lane and then follow the field edge to (8) where we do a left-right wiggle to reach the road corner by the Poachers Barn pub on Osgodby Lane. We continue down the road as far as the bend at (9) and here turn back right beside Manor Farm Cottages.

Going left-right-left at the farm, we stay on the track to the fork at (10) and here swing right to continue along field edges up the gradual rise of Knox Hill. There's a good view from the top of the hill as we descend to walk beside, and then across the golf course to College Lane (11). A right turn leads us to the A165 again; we cross and, bearing slightly to the right, walk down to the end of Wheatcroft Avenue before turning left back to our start.

Special Interest – WALK 29

In June 1993 the **Holbeck Hall Hotel** collapsed as the unconsolidated boulder clay at the top of the cliff slumped down to the shore below. The cliff has been subject to regular movement. The first recorded slip ('an earthquake') in South Bay was in 1737 when grazing cows were transported – unharmed – down the cliff. The 1993 landslide caused the cliff to move back 50m and resulted in an estimated 1 million tonnes of material being displaced and spread for 100m across the beach.

Stone: At the Holbeck car park is a memorial plaque commemorating the completion of the cliff stabilisation work undertaken after the 1993 collapse.

Imminent collapse on Lebberston Cliff

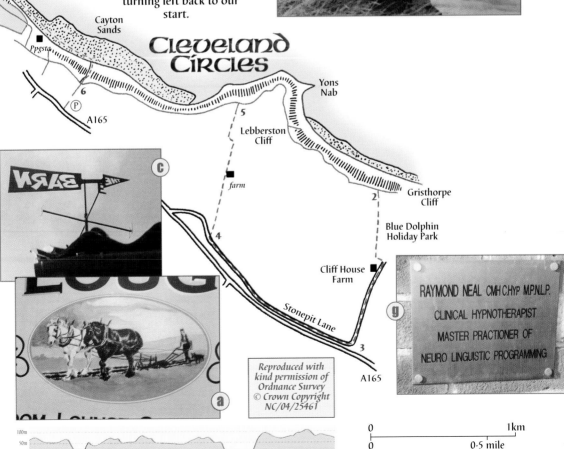

Osgodby Point

Cayton Bay

Cayton Sands

Ppgsta

Cleveland Circles

Yons Nab

Lebberston Cliff

farm

Gristhorpe Cliff

Blue Dolphin Holiday Park

Cliff House Farm

Stonepit Lane

A165

RAYMOND NEAL CMH C.Hyp M.P.N.L.P.
CLINICAL HYPNOTHERAPIST
MASTER PRACTIONER OF
NEURO LINGUISTIC PROGRAMMING

Reproduced with kind permission of Ordnance Survey © Crown Copyright NC/04/25461

100m
50m

0   1km
0   0·5 mile

WALK 30
GRISTHORPE CLIFF – FILEY

Map: Explorer 301
S.E.P.T.: North Cliff Country Park, Filey
      (121814)
Buses: 118, 119, 120, 121, 845, X45
      Rail to Filey
Cleveland Way distance: **2.7 miles**
Circular walk distance: **10.0 miles**
Shorter walk alternative: **6.8 miles**
Special interest:
    Filey Town Trail, Filey Brigg
Cross: Muston Cross (096796)

The last circuit finishes at Filey Brigg and allows the opportunity to explore Filey itself, making use of some of the excellent town trail information boards. We start from Filey's North Cliff Country Park and complete the circuit with the final CW section. There is no really satisfactory short circuit which includes the full stretch of the coastal path, though it is possible to use the road links shown on the map between Gristhorpe and Filey.

Setting off from close to the toilets at the Country Park, we skirt round the edge of the steep gulley leading down to the Sailing Club and then follow the cliff edge towards Filey; we are now on the Wolds Way/Centenary Way. When we come to the edge of Church Ravine, we turn right and, staying high above the steep slope, continue to St Oswald's Church (1).

Leaving St Oswald's we note information board 7 as we cross the footbridge over Ravine Road. We spot the well down to our left which stands on the site of one of the springs that used to supply fresh water to the town and to visiting Dutch fishermen. Continuing up Church Street, then turning left down Queen Street, we pass Filey Museum and at

the end of the street go down the steps to the seafront (2). We can investigate the Coble Landing to our left before continuing south along the promenade. Treasure hunters should stay alert as we follow the Filey Seafront Sculpture Trail.

There's another information board up to our right just before we pass the superloos and we can now start looking for some of the 50 silver flithers (limpets) hidden between here and the end of the seafront. When we come to Crescent Hill (3) we take either of the sets of steps up to Glen Gardens and at the top turn right and walk, parallel to The Crescent, through the Crescent Gardens as far as Belle Vue Street. Turning left, then first left again, we hurry past a magnificent

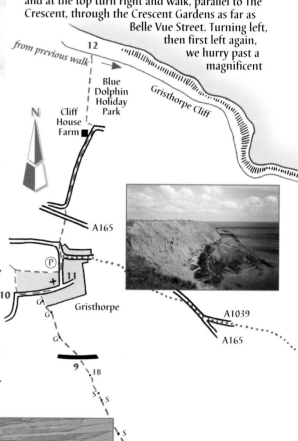

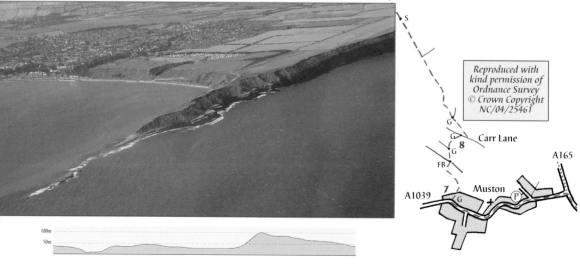

Reproduced with kind permission of Ordnance Survey © Crown Copyright NC/04/25461

vine and along South Crescent Road to Glen Gardens (4). This time we go across the park to the far left corner and descend the steps into Martin's Ravine. Spotting the giant ammonite to our left, we bear right to the steps on the other side of the ravine and go up towards the mini-golf course.

Our route on the Centenary Way bears left, and we now have the fence of the maxi-golf course on our right. Where the path splits (5) we fork right. Filey Golf Club's clubhouse soon appears on our left as we carry on along the gravel path, over the railway and on to join a tarred caravan park driveway. This leads us past two caravan sites to the A1039, just before which we catch sight of Filey's old windmill over to our right. We go left to the roundabout at (6) and then turning right and using the footpath by the roadside, we walk along the A165 until we turn off left on the A1039 again into Muston.

Keeping alert for treasure hunt clues, we walk through the village and, just before the end of the houses (7) turn right on the signposted footpath. Waymarks lead us on a rough track and then across one field and by the side of another, to the T-junction at (8). A right turn quickly brings us to Carr Lane where we turn back left and follow this p.r.o.w. for a little over a mile into Gristhorpe. At first the track is enclosed by hedges,

then we walk along the sides of cultivated fields. We need to take care crossing the railway at (9).

Entering Gristhorpe, we may wish to pay a quick visit to St Thomas' Church a short distance to our right but the main circuit turns left and continues to the road bend at the end of the village (10). Here we take the grassy bridleway on our right. After about 150m where the path bends left, we turn right on to another grassy path and walk behind the houses to the road at (11). Turning left, we soon come to Filey Road, bend left again and then almost immediately take the hedged path on our right that leads to the A165. Crossing over, we follow in reverse the route used on Walk 29 that takes us past Cliff House Farm and the Blue Dolphin Holiday Park to the CW above Gristhorpe Cliff (12).

There's now nearly three miles of glorious cliff scenery with which to finish the CW. As we pass the restored Filey Rocket Pole we are reminded of the courage and sacrifice of rescue workers who regularly risk their lives in the service of others.

At the CW marker stone the Trail officially ends but if time allows, there's the possibility of carrying on to the end of Filey Brigg before turning south and walking back to the Country Park car park.

Special Interest – WALK 30

Filey Town Heritage Trail links eight information boards that give a comprehensive summary of Filey's history and the route suggested for Cleveland Circles Walk 30 passes six of these notices. Near the start of our walk, Board 8 by the Country Park café tells us about the old open field system that used to operate in Filey as well as the development of Filey spa.

We should certainly make a point of visiting St Oswald's Church (there's an extremely helpful information guide) and then study Board 7 before taking the bridge over Ravine Road.

When we come down to the beach by the lifeboat station, we learn something (Board 6) about the history of Filey's fishing traditions. From records of disputes over the payment of fish tithes in the 12th century we can assume that fishing vessels have been working from Filey for more than 800 years. In mid-Victorian times the local fleet had more than 30 yawls and 70 cobles. Considering Filey never had a proper harbour, this was a surprisingly large fleet. Cobles were built on Coble Landing or on the foreshore. Yawls were built to stay at sea for several days and followed the autumn herring shoals as far south as Great Yarmouth.

Walking along the Promenade gives us a great excuse to dawdle as we admire the Seafront Sculpture Trail. Designed by Ross Coleman, this

includes a themed crazy golf course as well as a variety of imaginative features illustrating aspects of the town's maritime history.

As we turn up Crescent Hill, Board 4 tells of the importance of the sea-wall defences. These have protected the town itself but, as in other parts of the country, have deflected the sea's attack on to the unstable boulder clay cliffs on either side. In the shelter of Filey Bay the rate of erosion of the soft clay is estimated to be about 30cm a year. Whilst this obviously causes concern to home- and landowners, the rate is considerably less than on, for example, the Holderness coast where the cliff-line is exposed to the full force of North Sea storm breakers.

Continuing along The Crescent, we should not miss the 'Roman stones' on view near the bandstand. A landslide in 1857 on Filey Brigg exposed the foundations of what are thought to have been Roman buildings. It has been suggested that the

five large stones on display supported vertical oak beams that were inserted into sockets in the stones.

A little further on from the bandstand, Board 2 explains how in 1835 Filey's centuries old farming and fishing traditions were changed by the development of 'New Filey'. John Unett, a Birmingham solicitor, bought land, built The Crescent and provided Filey with what is generally agreed to be an extremely attractive piece of coastal architecture.

St Oswald's Church's present building dates from about 1180 and was probably founded by the Augustinian Friars of Bridlington who erected it on the site of an earlier Anglo-Saxon church. The original plan was to have included a west tower but this was never finished and so the structure is in two halves, the incomplete supporting pillars showing that the idea had been abandoned. In the bell chamber are two 17th century bells in addition to the new set of six lighter bells installed in 1981.

A new Church meeting room was opened in AD 2000.

Things to look for include:

- the excellent example of late Norman carving on the South Door which shows how the Normans had abandoned their previous chevron pattern in favour of continuous mouldings on rectangular facings
- the stone altar that was found in the middle of the floor where it is likely to have been placed at the Reformation when stone altars were taken down and laid on the floor for everyone to walk on
- the mass clock, indicating the times Mass would be said, cut into the south wall of the chancel
- the re-sited font which was originally covered and locked following an edict of 1216
- the 'Boy Bishop' carving that dates from around 1250. A boy bishop was selected by the boys of the parish to be their leader from St Nicholas' Day (6th December) until Christmas Eve. This effigy was almost smashed by a workman in the 1839 restoration but fortunately the bribe of a pint of ale was enough to stop him!

Filey Brigg's boulder clay 'badlands' are in danger of slumping away into the sea. However, a stroll from the Country Park along the top of Carr Naze makes an exhilarating addition to the Town Trail and the recently installed display boards give much detail about the geology and history of this part of the settlement.

Muston Cross plinth stands at the junction of West Street and Hunmanby Street and is now surmounted by a modern route direction post. A document dated 1203/4 mentions the deforestation of Hertfordlythe as far as the centre of Muston and the cross may have marked the boundary of the former forest.

TREASURE HUNT ANSWERS

WALK 1
(a) Helmsley car park (610838)
(b) Griff Lodge (590834)
(c) Rievaulx Bridge Cottage
(574843)
(d) St Mary's Church (577852)
(e) Gate on B1257 road (572873)
(f) Shop by car park (611839)

WALK 2
(a) Beulah House (533846)
(b/c) Ailred Barn (533846)
(d) Cottage (550860)
(e/f) Church (551859)
(g) Barn Close Farm sign (566855)
(h) Ashberry Farm (571844)

WALK 3
(a) Road junction (521829)
(b) Chapel Scotch Corner (527814)
(c) Main street Oldstead (531800)
(d) The Hare pub (549834)
(e) Leveret House (549834)
(f) Scawton Church (549836)

WALK 4
(a) Outside Visitor
Centre (516831)
(b) Inside Visitor Centre (516831)
(c) Memorial plaque (515828)
(d) Gatepost (502844)
(e/f) Steps at car park (515812)
(g) Glider warning (514813)

WALK 5
(a) Brickshed Cottage (468887)
(b) Kirby Knowle (469873)
(c) Church (468873)
(d) Boltby (489866)
(e) Boltby Churchyard (491866)
(f) Boltby (491866)

WALK 6
(a) Road mirror (465908)
(b) Obelisk (465906)
(c) Cowesby Church (464899)
(d) Datestone Cowesby (465899)
(e) Friar's Cross (488899)
(f) Cross Lodge (468917)

WALK 7
(a) Old School Over
Silton (451933)
(b/c/d) St Mary's Church (456932)
(e) Bird bath (456924)
(f) Nether Silton
carved post (456923)
(g) Boundary stone (480957)

WALK 8
(a) LWW stone by car park
(467992)
(b) Chequers (475971)
(c) Methodist church (457972)
(d) Bird mosaics
(e) Soldier
(f) Viewfinder Rueberry Lane
(453978)

WALK 9
(a) Gate by toilets (476021)
(b) Joiners Shop (478019)
(c) Private post-box (471012)
(d) Faceby Churchyard (496030)
(e) Whorlton Church (483025)
(f) Swainby School (478021)
(g) Swainby (1858) (478021)
(h) Swainby Church (478020)

WALK 10
(a) Boundary stone 'A' (511014)
(b) Spring at Lord
Stones Café (523030)
(c) Stone at Lord
Stones Café (523030)
(d) Viewfinder (535034)
(e) Gatepost (548028)
(f/g) Raisdale Mill (538005)

WALK 11
(a/b) Chop Gate car park (559993)
(c) 1826 date stone (559996)
(d) Stone water trough (548028)
(e) Marker post at road
crossing (573033)
(f) Foulis/Feversham BS
(alternative route) (581025)

WALK 12
(a/b) Ingleby Greenhow
Church (581063)
(c) Low Farm 'Stone
Circle' (585049)
(d) Hand Stone (595015)
(e) Red Stone (605015)
(f) Jenny Bradley
replacement (611023)
(g) Stoxley Stone (604042)

WALK 13
(a) Kildale garden (607093)
(b) Kildale Tea Garden (607094)
(c/d) Kildale Church (604096)
(e) 1668 gatepost
(former BS) (589098)
(f) Old cross in newer wall
(588096)
(g/h) Battersby Old Hall (596075)
(i) Topiary in Easby (577088)

WALK 14
(a) Notice board sign (592110)
(b) WB BS 1834 (593128)
(c) Tees Link (610137/604134)
(d) RIGS board (603134)
(e) Path up to Roseberry
Topping (581126)
(f) Summer House (577124)
(g) Plaque by path side (590102)

WALK 15
(a) Gateway to Gisborough Hall
(623160)
(b) Milestone on Whitby Road
(623160)
(c) C.S. marker post (616161)

(d) Music shop (616161)
(e) Seven Stars pub (615160)
(f) Bakehouse Square (614159)
(g) Mounting steps (615159)

WALK 16
(a) Fox and Hounds pub (643158)
(b) by Airy Hill Farm (646167)
(c) Skelton High Street
sundial (657188)
(d) Traffic island (655188)
(e) Barns Farm (647188)
(f) Methodist Chapel (632194)
(g) 10/V orienteering marker
(636202)

WALK 17
(a) Bench in Rifts Wood (663203)
(b) Bench in Rifts Wood (664207)
(c) Woodlands Centre (666208)
(d) Bandstand (666214)
(e) Burnside, on road to beach
(667216)
(f) Mortuary 1818 (669216)
(g) The Ship (670216)
(h/i) Symbols adjacent to
railway (695217)
(j) No. 9 Marine Terrace (713201)
(k) Coronation Street,
Carlin How (706192)

WALK 18
(a) 'Erato' plaque by road
bridge (714200)
(b/c) Tom Leonard Museum
(712192)
(d) Spring House Cottage gate
(745160)
(e) Swalwell Wood (731182)
(f) Loftus pub in High Street
(723182)
(g) Ladies P.C. (722181)
(h) Farm entrance (741192)

WALK 19
(a) Pub in Hinderwell (793167)
(b) By CW at Boulby (761191)
(c) Glen Dene (776179)
(d) Front garden in Cowbar
(781189)
(e/f/g) Houses in Staithes
(c.782188)
(h) 'Capt Cook's House' (783188)
(i) Dog Loup (783188)

WALK 20
(a) Anchor by car park (809160)
(b) Rocket pole (833158)
(c) Old entrance to rail
tunnel (838154)
(d) Goldsborough pub (836146)
(e) House sign (805159)

WALK 21
(a) Lythe Bank (856130)
(b) Lythe Church, outside
(850132)
(c) Lythe Church, inside (850132)
(d) Shell design on wall (861128)
(e) Whalebone arch (898115)

(f) Cook monument (898115)
(g) Newholm Hall Farm (877105)
(h) Beehive Inn, Newholm (867105)
(i) Coble Cottage (862125)

WALK 22
(a) Museum date stone (900110)
(b) Off Church Street (900112)
(c) Caedmon Cross (901112)
(d) High Hawsker (926076)
(e/f) Low Hawsker (925076)
(g) Sneaton toadstools (896077)
(h) Churchyard (894078)
(i) St Hilda's Church Sneaton (894078)
(j) Pavement decoration (899110)

WALK 23
(a) 1668 Mariners Tavern (953050)
(b) John Wesley memorial (953050)
(c) Marine Arts Centre (953049)
(d) End of the C-to-C Walk (953048)
(e) Flagstaff Steps (952048)
(f) Bird house (939052)
(g) High Mitten Hill Farm (920070)

WALK 24
(a) HD 1902 boundary stone (952009)
(b) The Range, Cook House (944007)
(c) Spring Hill Farm (940014)
(d) Harry's Folly (937018)
(e) Birdbath Ramsdale Mill Farm (926034)
(f) Ramsdale Mill (926035)
(g) House bell near Park Gate (937045)
(h) Middlewood Farm (945046)

WALK 25
(a) House by P.C. Ravenscar (980015)
(b/c) Hayburn Wyke Hotel (007969)
(d) Trough by road bend (996973)
(e) Island Farm (983983)
(f) Station Master (on gate) (975980)
(g) Hole in stone (979013)

WALK 26
(a) Crook Ness notice board (026936)
(b) Old Cloughton Station (011941)
(c) Oscar rail carriage (012941)
(d) Quarry Close Cottage (004939)
(e) Datestone (003939)
(f) Gatepost (981953)
(g) Moor to Sea waymark (978955)
(h) Standing Stones Rigg Farm (984969)

WALK 27
(a) Old Scalby Mills pub sign (036908)
(b/c) House names (014906/013906)
(d/e) St Lawrence Church (009903)
(f) Cumboots Farm gate (994911)
(g) Three Jolly Sailors pub (013929)
(h) Drive to Cliff Top House (024937)

WALK 28
(a) Top of Cliff lift (044876)
(b/c) Crown Hotel (043879)
(d) Rotunda Museum (043883)
(e) Gristhorpe Man (at museum) (043883)
(f) Cheapest Shop (046887)
(g) Anne Bronte's Grave (047891)

(h) By roundabout (Inner Wheel) (037896)
(i) Exit Peasholm Park (036896)
(j) Crazy Golf lighthouse (035904)
(k) Benny's Cave (048894)
(l) A.Castle & Sons (051888)
(m) Three Mariners pub (050888)
(n) King Richard III restaurant (049888)
(o) Pirate ship (048888)
(p) Scarborough 'Spaw' (045880)

WALK 29
(a) The Plough pub (079829)
(b) Bird house (056848)
(c/d) Poachers Barn (055847)
(e) Notice board – The University Of Hull (047865)
(f) Roadside water trough on A165 (047865)
(g) Nameplate in Wheatcroft Avenue (048865)

WALK 30
(a/b) Church Street Filey (117810)
(c) 54 Queen Street (118809)
(d) Promenade – Golf (120807)
(e) Promenade – Compass (120805)
(f) Promenade – Pavement (120804)
(g) Hotel sign (120803)
(h) Promenade – hopscotch (120802)
(i) St Mary's Church (118804)
(j) Crescent Bandstand (119804)
(k) Bronte house (118805)
(l) Ammonite (119800)
(m) Gristhorpe house date stone (086819)
(n) Christian fish symbol (985819)

IDENTIFICATION – CLEVELAND CROSSES & STONES

Key	Walk		
A	16	Skelton Cross	(655188)
B	17	Cleveland Coast marker stone	(671215)
C	18	Boulby Cliff trig. point 213m	(750195)
D	1	Helmsley Market Cross	(612838)
E	2	Sundial at All Saints Church Old Byland	(551859)
F	3	Cross base at St Mary's Church Scawton	(549836)
G	22	Caedmon Cross (either 901112 or 897101)	
H	23	Cross shaft in Low Hawsker	(923075)
I	24	Start/end of Lyke Wake Walk	(971012)

Key	Walk		
J	7	Cross remains in St Mary's churchyard	(456932)
K	8	Osmotherley old Cross shaft	(456972)
L	9	Bill Cowley memorial stone	(478005)
M	28	St Mary's Church Millennium Cross	(047891)
N	29	Holbeck Hall Hotel memorial stone	(049868)
O	30	Muston Cross	(096796)
P	19	Hinderwell War Memorial	(795165)
Q	20	Wade's Stone	(829144)
R	21	Restoration Mile Cross	(885110)
S	4	Cooper's Cross	(515829)

Key	Walk		
T	5	Kirby Knowle Church	(468873)
U	6	Steeple Cross	(495902)
V	25	One of the Three Lords' Stones	(969002)
W	26	Standingstones Rigg Small Stone Circle	(983970)
X	27	Millennium Cross at Scalby	(020904)
Y	10	Donna Cross	(545034)
Z	11	Wain Stone	(559035)
AA	12	Facestone	(597014)
CC	13	John Wesley plaque	(608094)
BB	14	Captain Cook's Monument	(590101)
DD	15	Guisborough Market Cross	(615160)

LANDSCAPES

Almost all the rocks of the North York Moors were laid down as sediments in the sea or in river deltas during the **Jurassic Age** (about 213 million to 150 million years ago). The only exception is the Cleveland Dyke (or Whinstone Ridge) that was injected as molten lava into the overlying rocks. The National Park Authority divides the Jurassic rocks into the following four broad groups, with the oldest rocks at the bottom of the table. This simple geological summary should help us to understand some of the major features of the landscape.

> **Kimmeridge Clay Group** – found in the Vale of Pickering, actually off the Cleveland Way
>
> **Middle Oolite Group** – including Calcareous grits and the Corallian limestone of the Hambleton Hills
>
> **Ravenscar Group (Deltaic Series)** – including the massive sandstones of the high moors
>
> **Lias Group** – including the Cleveland ironstone deposits and the jet and alum shales.

The Cleveland Way follows the edge of the North York Moors from Helmsley round to Filey. Along this route we pass through four different zones: the Hambleton Hills, the Cleveland Hills, a short stretch of the Cleveland Plain and the cliffs of the North Yorkshire coast. The circular walks that make up 'Cleveland Circles' allow us to venture off the National Trail and see a little more of these four landscapes.

The Hambleton Hills form the western edge of the North York Moors and run approximately from Helmsley to Osmotherley. The limestones and sandstones that make up the Hambletons are part of the Corallian division of Jurassic Age rocks that formed originally in warm, shallow water. Signs of former limestone quarrying activity can be seen at places like Kepwick. Limestone was quarried both for building purposes and to make into lime for use on farmland.

The rock dips gently eastwards and this produces the impressive escarpment that overlooks the Vale of York. This meant that the Hambleton Hills had a fine strategic position and so became a good location for settlement in prehistoric times and we see numerous reminders of those days as we follow the Cleveland Way. Today's village settlements, however, lie in a line at the foot of the steep escarpment where conditions are much less exposed than at the top of the scarp.

The Cleveland Hills make up the north-western part of the North York Moors and stretch roughly from Osmotherley to Guisborough. The surface rocks are mainly sandstones and gritstones of the Ravenscar Group. Here the terrain is more undulating than in the Hambleton Hills (and so more demanding for the walker) and the switchback section from Osmotherley to Clay Bank is regarded by some walkers as being the highlight of the whole Cleveland Way. The line of the scarp face, too, is less regular than earlier with the outliers of Whorlton Hill and Roseberry Topping and the deep embayment at Greenhow Moor creating a rather more varied cliff line. Along this section we see frequent reminders of the former alum, jet and ironstone mining activities that were at one time so important here.

The Cleveland Plain From Slapewath, close to Guisborough, the Cleveland Way descends to the built-up area of Skelton and then carries on to the North Sea coast at Saltburn-by-the-Sea. This short section of the National Trail is not as scenically attractive as the rest of the walk but it does give us a glimpse of the industrial heritage of Cleveland. Then as we leave Saltburn we scale the coastal cliffs and come to an altogether different landscape – the Heritage Coast.

The Heritage Coast stretches 36 miles (58 km) from Saltburn to Scalby Ness and is part of the longer Dinosaur Coast that runs from the River Tees estuary to Flamborough Head. The resistant Jurassic rocks are covered with boulder clay that was left by the ice sheets as they moved down from Scotland and across from Scandinavia. The unstable clay is easily eroded and regularly slumps down the cliff face as it did in 1993 when Scarborough's Holbeck Hall Hotel spectacularly collapsed.

Among the particular treasures of this stunning coastline is the wealth of fossils that are to be found. Observations of ammonites in the cliffs at Hummersea were of vital importance in the early development of geological dating techniques and at Kettleness ancient sea monsters like plesiosaurs, ichthyosaurs and crocodiles have left their marks. Further south on the rocky shores by Burniston and Scalby are the footprints of three-toed and five-toed dinosaurs.

Beyond Scarborough's South Bay, the Cleveland Way continues along the cliffs to end at Filey Brigg. This fine headland is made of very hard calcareous grit overlying a bed of oolitic limestone but at some time in the future it is likely to become separated from the rest of the mainland as the sea continues to hammer and erode the narrow neck of the promontory.

Today the coast is a rambler's paradise. But that has not always been the case – the quarrying of alum shales at numerous locations meant that places like Ravenscar and Sandsend were dreadful places and the scars of alum working still blight the landscape.